M000288833

# THE HEROIC

### AND

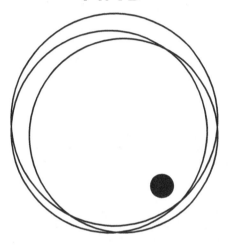

# EXCEPTIONAL MINORITY

## A Guide to Mythological Self-Awareness and Growth

*Gregory V. Diehl*

Copyright © 2021 Gregory V. Diehl

All rights reserved. No part of this publication may be reproduced, distributed, or trans-mitted in any form or by any means, including photocopying, recording, or other elec-tronic or mechanical methods, without the prior written permission of the publisher, except in the case of brief quotations embodied in critical reviews and certain other non-commercial uses permitted by copyright law. Any perceived slight against any individual is purely unintentional.

Although the author and publisher have made every effort to ensure that the information in this book was correct at press time, the author and publisher do not assume and hereby disclaim any liability to any party for any loss, damage, or disruption caused by errors or omissions, whether such errors or omissions result from negligence, accident, or any other cause.

The content of this book is for entertainment purposes only. Nothing found in this book is intended to be a substitute for professional psychological, psychiatric, or medical ad-vice, diagnosis or treatment. Neither author nor publisher accepts any responsibility for the results of any actions taken on the basis of information in this book. Author and pub-lisher expressly disclaim all and any liability and responsibility to any person in respect of the consequences of anything done or omitted to be done by such person in reliance, whether wholly or partially, upon this book. Always seek the advice of your physician or psychologist or other qualified healthcare provider with any questions you may have regarding a psychological condition. The information in this book is not intended to diagnose, treat, cure or prevent any disease.

For permission requests, write to the publisher at contact@identitypublications.com.

Library of Congress Control Number: 2021921579

Ordering Information: Quantity sales. Special discounts are available on quantity pur-chases by corporations, associations, and others. For details, contact the publisher at the address above.

Orders by U.S. trade bookstores and wholesalers. Please contact Identity Publications: Tel: (805) 259-3724 or visit www.IdentityPublications.com.

ISBN-13: 978-1-945884-21-4 (paperback)

ISBN-13: 978-1-945884-29-0 (hardcover)

Cover artwork by Resa Embutin (www.ResaEmbutin.com).

First Edition. Publishing by Identity Publications. www.IdentityPublications.com

Also by Gregory V. Diehl:
*Brand Identity Breakthrough* (2016)
*Travel as Transformation* (2016)
*The Influential Author* (2019)
*Everyone Is an Entrepreneur* (2022)

For those who are slowly or quickly realizing that there is something wrong with the world.

For those who accept that they can (and must) do what others cannot.

For my descendants, so that they may learn sooner than I did.

# TABLE OF CONTENTS

# FOREWORD

What makes up a hero?

The classic definition:

*"Heroism consists of putting others first, even at your own peril. The noun heroism comes from the Greek hērōs, which referred to a demigod."* [1]

Heroism is a challenging paradigm of many internal and external factors that, like exceptionalism, frequently depends on third-party views, evaluation, and practical proof over time and often in retrospect. To yours truly, for example, exceptional heroic aptitude transcends the self and is extended with compassion to all beings. It takes moxie and moral courage to accept obstacles and responsibility to act in the interest of a true common good.

Most human experiences are subjective. Inviting contrasting new perspectives to enrich the freedoms we enjoy is a prime, if not the pole, position for any tolerant, open-minded, and worldly person. And that's exactly where the distinct interpretations of exceptionalism and heroism in *The Heroic and Exceptional Minority* by Gregory V. Diehl come in.

His new book explores the notion of heroism within and mainly outside what's called Society. Through the prism of the unusual, complex, courageous, and most certainly exceptional man he is, Gregory outlines his tenets of *The Heroic and Exceptional Minority* and how they apply to you and the modern world. He speaks directly to a small group of self-aware people so different that they proudly accept to identify as anomalies to the norm. He declares and explains a state of self-chosen exceptionalism and its relevance to the individual via 20th-century-inspired mythological meta-human contexts, addressing the goals of self-actualization, finding strength, and being exceptional and even heroic. Gregory throws a proverbial gauntlet at the traditional narrative of how to define and even live heroism and exceptionalism through his exploration of the conditions and motives of aspiring outliers—a tantalizing inspiration to the different few who still linger in the social contexts of the normative many.

*The Heroic and Exceptional Minority* is a roadmap to discover an inner hero with the awareness of too often hidden and overlooked exceptionalism. Gregory's ideal of recognizing yourself as an upright person with heroic aspirations is a fresh, passionate, and unique approach to outstanding otherness. This liberating book is also about finding your feet when you're walking on quicksand and eggshells, limited and in discomfort with your environment. And it's about becoming an agent for the positive change you are missing in the world: A stimulating mental and behavioral concept that stems from Gregory's deep conviction, personal experience, and tons of self-efficacy.

---

[1] https://www.vocabulary.com/dictionary/heroism

How can we best create the reality we need to flourish for ourselves and others? By taking the liberty to be different and pursue goals that beckon beyond the norm. Gregory's notion to identify yourself as potentially heroic and exceptional, even before the fact, strikes as a sharp spark to become that and act accordingly one day, doing the right, the ethical thing, instead of being a limp onlooker or doing a runner whenever the going gets tough.

*The Heroic and Exceptional Minority* is a fascinating book that poses meaningful questions as to the relevance of and alternatives to the mainstream scope of life. It is *the* book for people that don't mind responsibility and constant reflection and those that hear the clarion call to conscious action by accepting an ever-uphill yet rarely glamorous path. It is a must-read for those that encounter the demanding traits of exceptionalism, who wonder about their role while surrounded by a non-chosen status quo and ponder their future options.

Being Gregory V. Diehl is no mean feat. I know what I'm saying since he and I look back on almost ten years of association, so… no mean feat at all. Hence, Gregory's *Heroic and Exceptional Minority* is neither an invitation on a wishful ego trip nor a soothing shortcut to feel elitist. It is not offering simple solutions or a self-congratulatory dose of projective Prozac to anyone seeking to just blame their respective environments for personal lack of meaningful character. Rather, treat it as your executive memo to rise, identify, and become your ultimate self by withstanding the tide of prescribed objectives and meet the challenge of a life lived for a consequential purpose. There is no promise of any reward other than respect for your choice to discover your *raison d'être*—the reason you are here.

Whether you are a young person at the starting line of your journey, a parent, a teacher, a mentor, or a guardian, this thought-provoking book will help you foster heightened understanding of the true nature of yourself or your protégées.

Helena Lind, writer and creator

> **Excellence is never an accident. It's always the result of high intention, sincere effort, and intelligent execution. It represents the wise choice of many alternatives: Choice, not chance, determines your destiny.**

Aristotle (384 – 322 BCE), Greek philosopher, from his Nicomachean Ethics

# IMPETUS

Since youth onward, I have never ceased noting that the ways of the world are, by and large, not remotely the same as my own. There was then and remains now a significant and unignorable difference in the domain of how we perceive who we are and how we ought to behave.

And so, I believed there to be something profoundly wrong with me for naturally operating so differently than the norm. Appropriately, my greatest existential dread has stemmed from my desire to resolve the impassible distinction I felt between myself and the world that I had no choice but to continue to be part of.

You might live burdened by similar feelings, including the perception that you need to pull away from your world because it does not seem to serve your development. You wish to discover more about yourself than your environment allows for. If so, it is likely that you will struggle, as I have, absent purpose, against barriers beyond your control.

If you should sit too long and rest too deep in mundanity, you will surrender to the entropy of your environment. You will submit to the world and allow it to mold your life into its quasi-comfortable patterns. You will begin to think things aren't so bad as you once imagined they were. You will convince yourself that you can endure the life not meant for you.

And that is why I felt the impetus to communicate: For you and countless others like us. For my children who do not yet even partake in the luxury of existing but will one day have the most important choice in the world to make and commit to, the choice to endure and remain good and true to themselves in a world that does not make it easy. That is, after all, the heroic principle in summary: To remain true to reality and self irrespective of the practicality, to use whatever power we have in the pursuit of doing good.

Goodness and power. Heroism and exceptionality. Such labels are commonly attributed by public interpretations of deeds performed or reputations spread according to the dominant values of the relevant culture in each moment. But there is an objective, absolute, and apriori kind of structure through which to analyze these important qualities well before and even forever absent celebration or approval. These words, like any other descriptors, represent categories of complementary qualities that will either be present or absent in any given individual. If present, the labels apply. If not, they do not.

Heroism always begins with examination of the self. A heroic person is one who seeks to know himself and, by extension, what will grant meaning to his experience of life. He refines his knowledge and abilities continually across time, casting out inadequate ideas as needed. He resolves his insecurities to better serve his values without hesitation or distraction. He does this so that he may determine his own destiny in lieu of letting his environment determine it for him.

As well, it extends outward into the environment. A heroic person, upon discovering his values, nurtures potential related to those values wherever he finds it, defending it against degradation or attack. He aligns his actions with moral values that apply objectively and absolutely because the effect he has on other people and his environment matters to him. Through this allegiance, he contributes to the moral and structural order of his world.

An exceptional person, meanwhile, is one whose prominent personality traits are not well-represented in his environment. He is extra-humanly abled in a domain of thought, perception, or action that is so extreme that it is likely unacknowledged and often even unwelcomed by the present world. Because of this, an exceptional person cannot effectively be categorized the same as his peers and, thus, struggles to function by the same standards and practices. Appropriately, he experiences intense frustration at the lack of opportunity to embody his nature and potential.

It is the rare and unfortunate combining of these two qualities in an individual that produces the greatest propensity for despair but also accomplishment should that despair be overcome. It is he who most needs the essential guidance of a type that is sorely lacking in the world.

# ORIGINS

◆—————•—————◆

## Mentorship and the Medium of Mythology

*"The real audience for all stories and all myths is the kids who are coming of age. We enjoy the stories as adults, but really, storytelling is about imparting the wisdom of the previous generation onto the children who are becoming adults and giving them a context for how to behave and how to learn the lessons of the past without making the mistakes on their own."*

— George Lucas

You may have never really struggled, in the traditional sense, to survive. Yet, for reasons you have not been able to fully identify, your discontentment with life steadily grows. You do not have the life you believe you ought to. You are not yet the person you feel you were meant to be, and the world never seems to work the way you think it ought to.

Every day, minds such as yours begin to suspect that the way they operate is distinct and set apart from the other minds of their reality. All existential progress, ultimately, rests upon this minority whose nature impels them to live beyond the norms of their societies. If they endure long enough, they cannot help but transform their environments.

Distinguished members of this exceptional minority realize early on that they have profound capacities for original thought and reflection, as well as an inherent need for meaning behind all their actions. But without guidance or a sense of belonging within their communities, they often languish over the perception that no one thinks or feels as they do.

Still, they are conditioned into tribes they never wanted. Their growth is bridled by the comfortable limitations of their peers and guardians. While individuals who are only marginally set apart may be celebrated for their differences, those who are far removed in their design will be cast out by others who cannot relate to them even a little. Such alien creatures have no ready place in this humdrum world.

Burdened by otherness, they begin to question their ability to ever find a fulfilling role in life. The estranged individual who lacks validation and undergoes isolation too long may come to question the merit of even continuing to exist at all. He will find it too painful to proceed through life alone, forever wondering if every inclination he has is acceptable and unable to identify with the popular values of the time.

Signs of exceptionality become apparent early in human development. The uncommon child may not play the same as ordinary children do. Strange objects, activities, and ideas might hold his attention to an absurd degree.

He may be oddly thoughtful, introspective, or even wise despite his dearth of experience.

Cultural authorities, feeling threatened by what they cannot understand or control, will most often undertake great efforts to curtail his abnormal behavior. If the exceptional child should not be allowed full, unbridled exploration of his differences, those differences may only become obvious later in life instead, when he has reached a state of greater freedom from direct coercive influence.

At the onset of puberty, when major biological changes coincide with shifted social dynamics, new modes and nodes of personality quickly develop. The mostly happy child who lived for more than a decade may quickly disappear, transforming into someone now contemplative and sullen. He feels this way because no one has ever shown him how to discover who he really is and how to be celebrated for it.

In other cases, the rare outsider who, against all pressure to change himself, somehow finds a way to embrace his underlying nature from youth onward soon becomes too much for anyone near to him to handle. They will urge him to sacrifice his development for the sake of their comfort. And so, he will soon realize that he is unlikely to ever bond with anyone quite like himself.

Yearning to belong, yet grappling with a profound sense of separation, the exceptional individual must either succumb to the pressures of conformity and be accepted or decide that alienation is a cost he shall willingly bear to flourish completely as himself. He can keep his connections at arm's length or incinerate them in the intensity of his being. He can maintain the present trajectory of his society or devote himself to growing beyond the limits of his birth.

A young adult, for the first time applying discretion to his own evolution, seeks out mentors suited to offer guidance for the challenges he faces. Good mentors naturally recognize young people who display uncommon brightness, ambition, and willpower. They offer the support to make it through difficult trials, passing on the lessons of their own experience integrated with timeless principles they have picked up along the way from universal sources. But anyone who does not understand the burden of not belonging in the world cannot offer insight about it, and so relevant and adequate mentors are more often than not difficult to come by when they are most needed.

Cultural mythology is mentorship that persists across civilizations and generations. It is timeless, containing the fundamental principles of human development within it. Our myths bind the alienated into a shared existential truth, finally providing a metaphysical community to belong to. Wisdom, dreamt up for as long as there have been human thinkers, moves across the thinking generations. Timeless ideas about how life works and how we ought to act populate our archetypal religious tenets, rules of etiquette, and unending variations on the same old parables and fables we tell ourselves to make sense of the chaos of living.

We, alive on the human Earth today, are privy to the most codified and concentrated structures of wisdom ever amassed, the ones that have somehow endured the thread of our ancestors until now. Mythology demonstrates something deep about the human experience. The narratives we relate to most are those that integrate into our identities, inspiring and molding our behavior in ways we are not always even conscious of. Our favorite stories are proxies for what we desire to become and do. The myths we connect to reveal principles we would otherwise miss within the span of our own solitary lifetimes. Mythology, not being subject to the same limitations as tangible reality, has been fine-tuned across innumerable retellings.

Reality's chaos, lacking a narrative structure, occurs randomly and arbitrarily. Purpose is impossible here without mythological structure because there are no means by which to measure the meaning of an action. Humanity's long-running narrative archeology reveals truths that everyday life could never do because their scale is too large and their conclusions unobviously emerging from the obvious properties of individual experience. Consequently, to exist at all, heroic mythology must appeal to our hidden internal motivators, forming the archetypes that proliferate throughout our history.

Many will live and die on this Earth without ever receiving the guidance they require to live up to their vast potential. There simply isn't enough of it to go around in human form. In light of this, perhaps it is our archetypal stories that have been principally responsible for supporting the ongoing existential evolution of humanity. Within the frameworks of our fiction, archetypal figures discover who they are through challenges tailored to their unique values, abilities, and limitations. The archetypes they represent are timeless because they coincide with the unchanging truths of human development.

The concept of a hero represents the overcoming of odds, adversaries, and adversities to accomplish something of deep personal importance. His quest is always to become an ever-better embodiment of his values, and, in doing so, he changes the very world itself to be more like him. Heroes, in any form, are idols we admire because they embody the virtues we wish we had the strength to call our own. Our heroes demonstrate our impossible ideals.

Within the storyworlds of fiction, characters have the luxury of being condensed into the core elements needed for their developmental arcs. Super-men and -women are written as concentrated masses of the greatest aspects of humanity, magnified via exceptional abilities and fantastical environments, maximizing their integration and influence. The most successful codifications become household names, their stories common knowledge around the world but their deep archetypal truths about the human condition still most often taken for granted.

I, a boy developing affinity for the cinema of my era, noted that (but did not fully understand why) most new stories were entertaining for a time and then quickly lost their interesting qualities with repeated exposure. However, I realized even then that a select few had qualities that made my capacity to enjoy them and derive meaning from them increase with each new exposure. I was experiencing the story as a whole, analyzing and appreciating each change that occurred scene by scene for its significance in the context of the whole. I realized that some stories were about more than the events that transpired around their protagonists; they were about the principles that would reflect my own inevitable experience.

In *The Lion King*, I saw young hero-in-the-making Simba fall from his preordained path of royalty into an idle and hedonistic existence, free of worry, responsibility, and meaning. But Simba's origins inevitably caught up to him, reminding him of his real identity and destiny. Simba was made to reflect upon his rightful place in the world and fight to reclaim the responsibility he once ran from. By willingly taking the burden of his own existence and the order of his environment (i.e., accepting his place in the circle of life and all its consequences), Simba brings the influence of heroism to a reality that fell into utter disorder without it.

*Star Wars* offered me, at first as a young boy with the original three movies and then later as a teenager when the newly released prequel trilogy concluded, dual heroic arcs turning away from each other at their most defining moments. Anakin Skywalker, lacking sufficient mentorship, succumbs to his unresolved dark emotions. Luke, his unknowing son, embarks upon a similar path a generation later. Through the interjection of now-wiser versions of his father's old mentors, Luke, at last, receives guidance that is relevant and adequate for the completion of his path to heroism. Luke's success holds true to his chosen values in the face of great temptation, possible only through the perspective of his father's prior failure, demonstrating that a villain is frequently a failed hero at his core.

Most quintessentially, the transcendent story of Superman (however endlessly recreated across comics, television, and major motion pictures for the last three-quarters of a century) portrayed for me the timeless pattern of an unconfident and alienated wanderer who, despite his obvious natural advantages, must gradually grow into acceptance of his identity and design. Clark Kent, the masquerade of mediocrity, cannot deny the truth of his exceptionality forever. He must choose to remain hidden among the ordinary or embrace his great potential and all its implications. Resolving this internal paradox, often through the influence of the woman who loves him for who he really is, raises Clark out of obscurity and onto the world's stage as Superman, self-realized paragon of heroic ideals, at once walking among and soaring above humanity.

Superman's status as mythological inspiration and a map for other exceptional beings to follow is so secure in human culture that it has even reached meta-mythological levels. The story of Superman is functionally now a mythological influence to heroic characters within other stories that are meant to serve as mythological influences to us real-world humans. His seems to be a sort of prime contemporary hero story from which other contemporary hero stories emerge and draw their influence.

In the animated movie *The Iron Giant*, an alien weapon in the form of a towering metal robot arrives on Earth for the purpose of destruction. However, it befriends a young boy, one who, critically for the story, has retained the naïveté, idealism, imagination, and optimism that is characteristic of youth. The boy offers a mythological education of sorts to the giant by introducing him to the Superman comic books he loves and relating the superpowered alien orphan's story to the giant's own. And though it was designed for an entirely different purpose, the giant soon gains the ability to choose a higher-order destiny for itself and become a protector of humanity, all due to the inspiration passed into it by the new narrative of Superman it has been exposed to and the boy's earnest belief in it.

This connection is not implicit or accidental. The giant even goes so far as to affix a red S to his extended chest and place his hands on his hips in imitation of his hero's signature pose. Later, upon learning to fly, the giant holds his arms in front of him just like his meta-mythological mentor. His dying word at the climax of the film, "Superman," is the explicit reminder of precisely what enabled him to make the once-impossible choice to sacrifice himself for humanity instead of succumbing to the pre-existing pressure to destroy it.

Within the storyworld of *The Iron Giant*, the titular giant becomes the equivalent of the real-world embodiment of the heroic values that Superman is supposed to represent. The giant's choice, in turn, penetrates one level deeper into our real world by inspiring and reminding us that we too can become the heroic, ideal versions of ourselves, so long as we are convicted enough to ignore what path societal influence (whether of human or robot alien origin) would otherwise pressure us onto.

The fundamental difference between stories and reality is that stories (good ones, anyway) are composed exclusively of meaningful elements. They are crafted according to the omniscient perspective of a storyteller with goals and values he wishes to imbue onto his manufactured universe. Reality has no inherent order or meaning beyond what its physical laws constrain it to. But a narrative is defined wholly by order and significance. It has no disconnected parts that putter about in unplanned directions for no real reason.

Our mistake is unconsciously expecting reality (and, more specifically, the courses of our individual lives) to play out according to the artificially imposed structures of meaning we find in every great story ever told. Every culture's foundation of ongoing narration creates expected norms and patterns for how every conscious pursuit ought to go, dictating what our personal life adventures should always be like. So, in a certain sense, they become self-fulfilling narratives. Accepting that they are how reality works makes us act in such a way upon the portion of reality over which we have influence that it begins to conform to them.

Our shallowest hero stories portray goodness as merely a base ingredient in righteous people. Heroic acts go unexamined because they require no reflection or inquiry beyond merely being the accepted premises of their stories. Such stories offer nothing to real-world outliers struggling with their roles and values in the world as it really is. Heroism embodied in the flesh is a choice arrived at solely through introspection about one's place in the world and the nature and impact of one's actions.

Heroic goodness depends upon the acceptance of the idea that existence can be meaningful and that how we behave contributes meaningfully to the world we are part of. So, a true, real-life hero molds himself to become the embodiment of what he wishes for the world. He holds himself accountable to the standards he applies to the rest of humanity. A hero is someone who has learned to live in alignment with his values, regardless of the world's expectations, to the point that he is willing to undertake great hardship, risk, pain, and maybe even death to uphold them in the portion of reality he considers his domain.

For fictional narratives to function, characters must be codified into their base defining elements. They are concentrated masses of the most important aspects of humanity, magnified through extraordinary conflicts and abilities. Though popularly seen as opposites, codified heroes and villains exhibit many similar traits, even to the point that they are often both willing to die for the causes they believe in. But a hero is determined to reflect on the total nature and impact of his actions. He must be certain that the meaning behind his actions and their consequences is in alignment with the order he is trying to enact into the world. For him, there can be no disingenuousness or incongruity.

A hero, never sure of the rightness of any of his individual actions, takes time to reflect upon his failures and successes. A villain does not. A hero seeks an intimate relationship with reality. Justice is how he restores order to his world. A villain takes the impatient path toward immediate emotional resolution. He does whatever he perceives will make him feel better and compensate for his emotional insecurities. His moral failings compound into a torrent of aberrant and irredeemable behavior until he has lost all perspective on the real nature of his role.

If our timeless narratives exist to symbolically reflect reality and guide us through the challenges that surpass the purview of a single human lifetime and fill the vital roles of the mentors we are likely to be lacking, how could they ever lead us astray or fall short of bringing us to our ultimate destinies? Why does it often seem like there is such an incongruence between our favorite stories and how reality actually goes without regard for our expectations?

One explanation is that our common story archetypes, such as the classic "hero's journey," represent reality unfolding under ideal conditions, immune from the chaotic interference of a thousand ever-present unknown variables. They show us what can happen if everything goes according to plan once we step outside our comfort zones and pursue some meaningful goal despite encountering challenges and obstacles. Stories are sequences of meaningful transformation in a vacuum and, as such, retain a level of purity that only principles can because they are not bound to the chaos of our physical reality. Unlike a story we've heard, read, or watched a thousand times over, none of us can ever know reality perfectly and completely. Thus, even under the best of conditions, reality is necessarily always chaotic.

Now, more than ever, we are free to go, willingly into the unknown, to explore new worlds, and to present our experiences as meaningful archetypal journeys – to conquer reality's chaos. All who are aware that they feel the ambition from childhood onward to accomplish exceptional tasks and mold their lives according to their own values, lives worth telling about, can pursue that meaning in whatever ways are most appropriate for them. Yet, still, the outlier who ignores cultural expectation or convention to pursue what is enduringly right stands out as awkward and unrelatable under the overbearing perception of the ordinary.

The hero of myth and legend always has a meaningful, transformative arch by the end of his story. Real life does not allot such predefined paths to follow. Past a certain point in the journey, there are no further mentors or gurus, whether actual or fantastical, to chaperone our heroic development. No human has taken the necessary next steps in a specific journey. So, the real-life hero discovers what he is made of in a vacuum, isolated from societal interference, left only to his own devices to discover what is left of him when he has surpassed all around him. Only then does he carve out a footing from which to operate in the world, to change both himself and his portion of reality to the higher standard he can tolerate.

The pertinent thing to keep in mind about our fictional myths of heroic and exceptional people is that they represent the real qualities contained by every good person who strives to make his actions meaningful and constructive. Every villain, alternatively, belongs to the overlap of categories of actions that people who are hurt, fearful, embittered, and insecure take to manifest their antagonism against the overarching order that is, in spite of their efforts, still slowly making its way into the world. The choice between those two extreme ends is the most important choice in the world for the individual who struggles with what to make of his time here on Earth and what to do with the staggering potential he suspects he holds.

Perhaps the chapters that follow will do some small amount to help you and others like you commit and stick to the positive path, despite all the reasons there seem to be to take the opposite route or abandon the quest entirely. Support is necessary because the path described here is guaranteed to be composed of moments that will not be easy to endure. Struggle is inherent to it. Suffering is inevitable for a heroic person because he is defined by expectations that surpass the capacity of his world to meet. Pain is actually essential to the process because it anchors him in the truth and helps him focus and remember when all the world applies its pressure to forget the path after any major breakthrough and return to its fold.

Readers would be wise to take all presented here with a serving of salt and ignore any words that do not align with their own experience of reality and self. None of it is intended to convince you of anything that does not ring as true in your observations of your place in the world or change you from what you are.

As well, what I have to say is not advice for those seeking glorification through their actions or worldly identities. Those who, under the influence of their souped-up vanity, lust after narratives of self-indulgent and super-ficial importance are already acting incompatibly with reality and heroism as outlined in what follows. It is not a destination anyone strives to arrive at through the promotion of their own narrative or social fanfare. It is the unfortunate curse of having been born with a nature that guarantees lamen-tation for lack of a proper place to live here.

This is not merely about control. Conviction and the ability to determine your own destiny per se are not what make for heroism. A truly heroic person would never feel the need, for example, to force other people to see things his way or act in accordance with whatever limits he has decided are appropriate for them absent their agreement. He seeks to raise up the weak, not hold them down for the unstated purpose of making himself seem higher.

Many exceptionally awful people have been those who pursued great ambi-tions and attempted to shape the destiny of their world in the image of their values. But their lack of an absolute sense of moral responsibility that applies categorically in all situations turned their great potential sour. They created arbitrary divisions between people and situations that only served their own insecure emotions and the agendas that followed. They were so desperate to resolve the consequences of their core inadequacies that they refused to consider the totality of the impact of their existence, the premises behind and logical consequences of how they applied their will on the world. What-ever they might have claimed when the lights were trained and the cameras were rolling, their true motivation was never to improve and bring objective peace to the world. It was always to achieve a fleeting sense of superiority, importance, and control to compensate for what they were not able to create within themselves.

For someone to be truly heroic is to be unignorably impelled by his own nature toward actions that contribute to a higher state of moral order in his environment – not by seeking to dominate the wills of others he considers to be inferior but by inspiring and building the superior state of things that he envisions. The strength of his despair and the conviction stemming from it must be filtered through an absolute and objective sense of permissible behavior. His role exists irrespective of social accolades for whatever is con-sidered worthwhile in the eyes of the majority, which is often little more than villainy with an attractive face or a celebration of surrender. He will know who he is by the call he feels to do what he must to further his own develop-ment, even long before he consciously understands where that development will take him. He starts because he must, because to do anything else would be to submit to self-destruction.

# 01
# Disappointment and Start

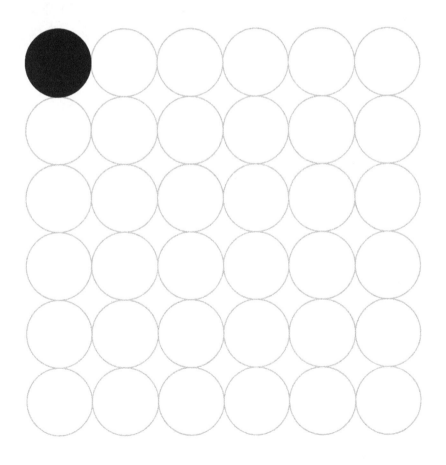

# Disappointment and Start

*Any heroic journey begins with the realization that reality is not how the ideal-ist mind, for some unexplored reason, feels that it should be. From that initial awareness, countless unknown and attractive possibilities lying just outside what is familiar branch outward. We see now that what we know does not offer the crucial sense of purpose that we have started to realize we are missing. Now, at last, it is more favorable to brave the unknown than to remain where we had prematurely settled, and our journey at last initiates.*

The question of the nature of one's own identity is one of the most ordinary questions in the world, yet few of those who ask it ever realize how much a meaningful answer would really matter. People are accustomed to only su-perficial responses that serve no function except to put into words the most basic personal descriptors about themselves. Because of this, it is easy to for-get that the stories an individual tells himself about who he is represent only a fraction of the ways he could ever arrange himself. His answers are limited to what he has so far been able to experience of his own nature and potential.

Through one path or another, all people have no choice but to live out the destiny they set for themselves through their recurring self-narration. But what defines a person at his core is not set by the place he was born, the way he was raised, or the mundane activities that pilfer his time. The person who feels that he has been told whom to be needs not limit his ability to be whomever he feels most determined to become. But if such a person fears what he will find when he peers inside himself, he will linger in the safety of expectation. Such a person dies never knowing who he really is and what he could have accomplished had he had the courage to act on his own interests.

Meaningful self-conception only begins with a sense of distinction from the rest of society. People seek out complementary differentiation. The other people they know form the boundaries to their uniqueness. They find defi-nition through comparison to an arbitrary other, and, without meaningful social distinction, they feel formless and devoid of worth. This crippling need to affirm identity via society is a source of lifelong suffering. Without constant reiteration of who the wandering person is supposed to be in the world, the story everyone agrees to tell about him slowly fades. In its place, a void remains to be filled by dominant social influence.

Whenever we are unsure of ourselves, it is only natural that we should call upon our pasts to remind us who we are supposed to be and tell us how to act in uncertainty. Our established selves are constants we believe we can rely on in an ever-changing universe. We are afraid of what happens when we act outside our known parameters. But beyond our familiar conceptions of identity lie countless unexplored impulses and ambitions. Our insecure need for certainty is what prevents us from ever fully knowing them.

As an ordinary mind never ponders the truth of its own identity for longer an occasional clear and inspired moment, the world is quick to offer us a thousand easy avenues through which to evade introspection when it calls. Since we have no external reasons to change ourselves once any particular situational agony is over, we may never come to know our own deep sorrow, ambition, or nagging drive to move against the impassible.

Only if we are determined, if we have allowed ourselves to become so disappointed that no other choice remains but to purge our inauthentic self-conceptions, can we explore what we will become without a lingering past to define us. The longer we wait, the more resistance there will be for any emerging personality traits to encounter. The people who know us to be a certain way may feel betrayed and cheated by our sudden transformations. We may even face resistance from our own minds when the way we are used to thinking about ourselves attempts to defend itself from annihilation.

Yet, suppose we survive these social and psychological ordeals. In that case, it is possible for us to embrace the entire range of what we can become, delving deeper into what is valuable and discarding all the rest. Every latent interest yields possibilities to develop throughout our lives. If we unravel the restraints we know about ourselves, we can arrive at many contextual identities to embody. Then we will begin to discover what matters to us and defines us on our own time and in our own way.

You can't know what you really are until you've tried to become more than what you know yourself to be. So, you must develop the courage to do something that scares you, something you believe may even destroy the you that you know, something that seems entirely antagonistic to the identity you've assumed and utterly outside your limitations. Only when you survive the seemingly impossible do you enhance your understanding of the breadth of your own existence. Revel in small victories for a time, and then pursue the impossible once more.

Counterintuitively, growth often begins with removal and construction with deconstruction. Creation requires deletion. You must, in a sense, kill your old self before you can become your new self. So, in every moment, be willing to deconstruct the self-conceptions that prevail in your mind. Follow that thread of inquiry until the unrealized possibilities weigh heavily upon your soul. Then, no matter the cost, press on and embody the parts of yourself for which emergence is painfully overdue.

Begin by removing all but what is absolutely necessary from your ongoing self-reflection. Reduce everything in your emotional awareness to its simplest possible state. Release any demands from your attention that do not require your conscious input. Observe what remains. Rest there until something real beckons your motion once more. Do not turn away from the emptiness that appears when there is no emergency to stamp out or pressing pain to remedy. See what becomes of your thoughts when there is nothing to tell you what to do or become.

Waste no energy upholding outdated structures or values solely because you are accustomed to their bounding influence. When you are finally free from the confines of your traditional self, your society will be forced to choose how it will adjust to the effects of your now-expanded boundaries. The portion of reality you once called home may now see you a foreign invader adorning a once-familiar face. That is the risk you take when you break with your past for the sake of what your future may hold. Get on the path as early as you can, while there is time to act and you have the strength to initiate the changes required by heroism.

# 02
# Character and Upbringing

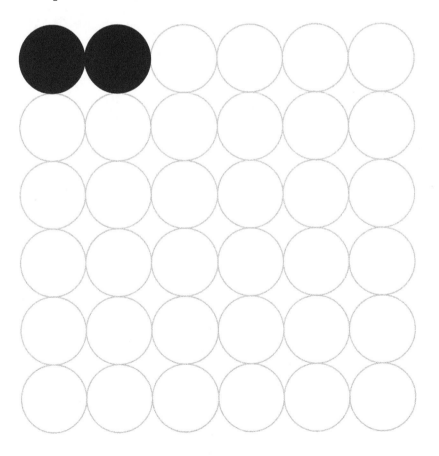

# Character and Upbringing

*All people begin life naïve and immature. From that early underdeveloped perspective, we cannot imagine all the terrible or incredible things that may occur outside the confines of where we start. Our early comfort is the prison that keeps us from realizing our potential. We must impel ourselves to depart from the world we know so that we may gain the perspective to reconsider the incidental and formative patterns of our youth. Then, we might begin to discover the lives we should have been living all along.*

As the start of every path, childhood prepares the young to thrive within their modern states of culture and technology. Their world was shaped by the elders who came before, who themselves only changed things from the conditions of those before them. Childhood is the stage of development that exists to teach children how to get along in the world as it happens to be at the time they are alive in it. For that reason, it has the capacity to be very harmful or misguiding to the young. The way it goes is a reflection of the ways of the world.

Children are more sensitive to change than at any other time in their development, as they have not yet uncovered the competence to process their natural emotional variance. The unavoidable dips and peaks in their moods reveal their range of possible responses to experience. The weight of early observation lingers long because young minds have not learned the difference between the harmful, the helpful, and the irrelevant. Many adults, in fact, never learn with precision how to make this critical distinction.

Every detail is both novel and important. A child has no perspective for any other way things could be than how they are or how he ought to feel about what is. There is not yet any internal database or filing system to refer to. So, his fresh perspective imposes a baseline against which all forthcoming experience shall be filtered. The responsibility of this natural fact is rarely fully understood.

Reality is positively loaded with wonders, terrors, and things unimaginable to childish minds, but its greatest dangers have been mitigated by countless forms of caretakers. An ordinary child is one who has never failed in any manner not allowed for by his overbearing guardians who spare him the risk of consequence or grave danger. Likewise, he has never run headfirst into his own ignorance or limitations because there have always been safeguards to prevent him from learning the truth about the nature of his actions. An immature mind, therefore, cannot predict the depth or breadth of what it might mature into. Minds more developed have taken great care to protect it from what they believe it is not yet ready to know.

However, in adolescence, a child's ambition may grow beyond what his guardians can effectively curtail. The new adult will finally operate outside the constraints he inherited and, for the first time, be subject only to what reality herself will or won't allow of him. Society's caretakers have not pre-

7

pared him to explore a world where he cannot easily distinguish what will hurt or aid him. And as such, he does not even really know what he wants or is capable of.

Without conscious interruption in the chain of consecutive limitations, we are at risk of recreating all our formative limitations, even well past the stage where our childhoods have ended. Our adult minds settle into believing that they already know what they need and, therefore, always will. Basic survival does not concern us as comfortable grown-ups who do not fear how we will make it through each day, so neither learning nor unlearning remain a major part of our priorities. The ideas we adopted before we knew to investigate them stay with us the rest of our lives as our silent, unconscious compasses.

Now, as mostly developed adults, it takes more effort to feel the same reactive emotions we did when we were young, when all was fresh and novel. Now, we've been around too long. Everything seems routine, a mild variation upon a familiar pattern. So, we hold our most potent childhood memories, whether traumatic or empowering, as sacred in our hearts because we don't know who we are without them. To glorify our upbringings as doctrine like this is a subtle form of narcissism. We believe the reason our memories matter is they are ours and not someone else's. We believe, without the warranted amount of self-reflection, that our lives are more true, more meaningful, and more important than the lives of others. We deem our experiences absolute and our interpretations universally valid.

We should beware those youthful associations that still maintain the power to hijack our emotions in the present. Unearned nostalgia can poison momentum and resolve, placing permanent caps on what we will become with what life we have left. If we accept that our best, most-defining moments are already behind us, we have nothing left to build and nowhere left to aim. If we lament old traumas long after they're done, we cannot help but recreate them. All progress becomes impossible, so long as we hold our childhoods sacred. Our perhaps once-healthy childhood limits do not serve our exploration or development any longer. They are now only barriers to self-knowledge. If development stops here now, we will remain mental children forever, navigating an increasingly complex world in adult bodies housing hobbled minds.

Because it is always easier to repeat what you know, you will, at first, look to the past for guidance about what's next in your path. You are predisposed to the familiar and not ready for the burden of the unexplored. You are not yet open to the idea that there are truths about you that you have never once been allowed to consider by those who set your limits. The arbitrary past is your anchor to how reality works and who you are permitted to be within it. Your goal now should be to figure how to change the way you think about the importance and events of your past.

No matter how much you learn about yourself and how many victories over the unfamiliar you accumulate, you cannot change the facts of your personal history. Only your interpretation of the past is fluid. It is a narrative you tell yourself, built from unreliable impressions at a time your mind was barely even aware of itself. Your understanding of your roots is masterable, capable of being endlessly rewritten if you know what you are doing. In embracing this fact, you will advance to superior trials, heal from superior traumas, and test your expanded self in much larger arenas.

Whatever it is that happened to you when you were young, however terrible, wonderful, or once-defining, does not have to matter any longer. Immature impressions should not follow you unless they are somehow aiding you in your trials in the present. The memories collected in early years, though probably not completely discarded, should be perpetually tempered by fresh eyes and experience. This is easy, so long as you are not afraid of letting go of your associations of who you once were. As you take in new information, you must clear the necessary space for that information to incubate and inform your awareness.

Upon realizing the particularly restrictive nature of your upbringing, you may feel you have lost your most important years in a prison the world built to encapsulate your childhood paradigm. Remember, though, that your authentic self was beyond the understanding of the world that reared you. It was reliant on the same social structures that conditioned it in raising you. Understanding that this is the way it is for nearly everyone, that your unaware caretakers acted the only way they could have within the confines of their conditioning, will make it easier to move on from your remorse about your upbringing.

And when you have finally disregarded what is inaccurate, inauthentic, or simply not useful about your childhood, you can take the reins of what you will become and optimize whatever happened to have been good about your character formation in upbringing. Whatever real things you learned about yourself back then may continue to hold a place in your identity—not because the world told you that you must keep them but because you have weighed their merit against the reality that unfolds a little more before you every day and seen their lasting mythological value.

# 03
# Goodness and Motivation

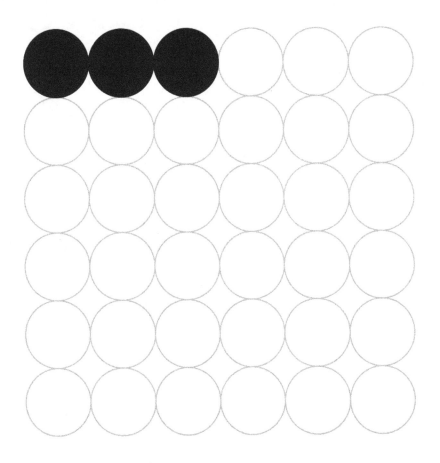

# Goodness and Motivation

*Narrative continuity in life stems from the act of aligning actions with values across all levels of analysis. We cannot be champions, cannot know what we are willing to fight and die for, what struggles will grant us purpose and reward, until we have examined our deepest internal motivators. Our moral principles are the source of our determination, so it is imperative that we discover what they are before making major choices about the moral character we will display in the world.*

There exists an intrinsic tendency to emulate whatever human behavior persists in one's surroundings at the time they first become aware of themselves. Social mimicry enables a young person to thrive throughout the systems others built for him, which he now depends on for survival. His necessary participation in them, in turn, ensures their proliferation and the continued need for them in generations to come. But if people cannot outgrow their institutional behaviors, new lives will always be the same as old ones, with always the same goals and limitations.

What a person does, however, upon establishing his own agency, depends on what really motivates him. Once he knows what he cares about more than anything else, he can make the choice to pursue it, even when the world is against him. By pushing himself to operate outside his known parameters and inherited limitations, he can look past the superficial values that have always been there in the forefront of his attention. Their removal is necessary to make space for his own priorities.

But it is impossible for anyone to investigate every expression of their values within the boundaries of a lifetime. There is too much to know about oneself, and the work required to know it is too great. Therefore, no matter how a person spends his time, a great portion of him remains undiscovered. Furthermore, the longer his life persists, the more incentive he will need to explore his still-unrealized potential. His strength will diminish with time and the ongoing march of entropy.

Motivation comes in many forms, and it evolves with the stages of human development. All people want many things, each of which competes for their limited attention, and many of which appear incompatible with each other. So, all people must be able to monitor the emotional weight they assign to each desire. When they understand their deepest motives, they will structure their time appropriately, never betraying who they are in following a want.

The world shall never hesitate to bombard its champions with its own priorities. It seeks out cracks in an open mind to enter and assimilate. If we are not strong and self-reliant, we bend to the world's influence without even feeling it. If we are not mindful of our own motivations, they get overtaken by countless others. So, to serve our values, we must grow able to plant ourselves firmly against prevailing social doctrine, standing proudly as the characters we know we are.

Each of our own lives takes its own course, starting with reflection upon who we are and moving outward from there. We need neither permission nor convenience to begin the inward search, only the longing to know what inspires us to pursue a fulfillment deeper than placation. The values derived from our environments are products of an amalgam of minds operating for shallow purposes. They are not the hard-won rewards of victory over internal conflict.

There will always be obstacles, tangible or not, on the path to what we desire. This resistance forces us to ruminate, as never before, on why we strive and whether such struggles are worth the hardship they inflict on us. Confronting our failed ambitions makes clear to us our real priorities. Unrealized expectations teach us about ourselves in ways we could never learn from always getting what we long for.

If we live our lives chasing faulty motivations, we can only ever develop a short-term view of our fulfillment. We will soon become trapped in a loop of alleviating one immediate pain after another, a hedonic circuit of shallow wants and meaning. We will build no great ambition and, therefore, face no chance of real hardship or failure. Because we are unwilling to march consciously toward our own meaningful suffering, we never self-reflect. We are still missing the critical ingredient to purpose.

Only when all familiarity and convenience disappear will we consciously assess what we are willing to endure for the possibility of resolving the deeper, existential lackings that rest deep beneath our surface wants. Introspecting into the nature of what really has the power to zap the meaning from our lives will call into question the validity of the paths we are on. Are we doing what we are for our own fundamental reasons? Or are we still stumbling in futility after the disappointment of yet another fleeting pleasure?

You do not have to float through life idle and self-stimulating as it is so acceptable to do in the world. As a motivated person, you may apply your unfulfilled desires as fuel to become more than your society condones of you. The ever-present awareness of your real motivations, including the potential for unhappiness they carry, creates a better model for you to evaluate the meaning of your life. Meaningful pursuits will offer you the respite you seek from the unbearable weight of your own mundanity. Whether you ever reach your intangible ideal, meaning resides in the growth that accompanies the effort of trying.

You may have not yet realized that there exists a thread connecting your most joyous moments to your most devastating. There is consistency between what you find most and least meaningful across the whole of reality. Something about the range of your responses remains valid under the most positive and negative ends of your experience. Realizing why you react so strongly to some things and not at all to others is key to uncovering your inherent and immutable motivations.

Someday, you're going to have to decide what you want and build your life around it. If what you want does not align with justice, your wants will be

forever at war with your growth as a heroic entity. As your behavior grows more consistent with your values, there will be fewer discrepancies between the pleasurable and the meaningful, and you will never have to sacrifice what matters for what feels good because you are desperate for distraction. Eventually, what matters is what feels good to you.

So, do what you can to gather a palette of experiences while you are young and able, for it is only when you have seen enough of the possible arrangements of life that the factors necessary to your fulfillment become clear. When you look back over the influential moments of your life, you will begin to decode their patterns. You will identify the determinants of your fulfillment and apply those principles to the ongoing structure of your life. Every possession you acquire, every relationship you forge, and every quest you undertake will service your development.

# 04
# Naiveté and Idealism

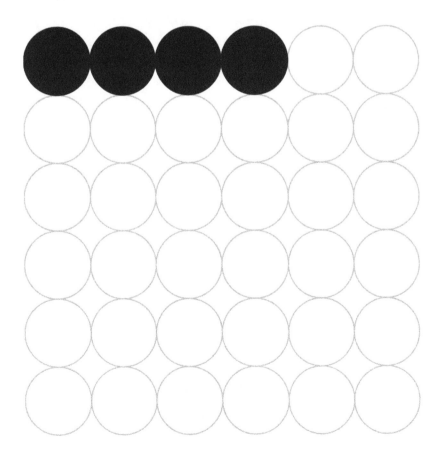

# Naiveté and Idealism

*It is the nature of those who see the way things could be to expect them to simply be that way without obstacle and to quickly grow frustrated when they are not. Such a way of living in the world as this leaves us vulnerable to rapid disillusionment regarding our values. Furthermore, it makes it easy for people operating with bad intentions to take advantage of our distant vision by making us ignore what is right in front of us. So, we must somehow find a way to turn this heartbreaking part of us into a source of momentum for our dreams.*

The hero, unbeknownst to himself or to anyone else at the start, is born into the world with a set of unexplored expectations about how it ought to work. He holds this naïve anticipation because he has prematurely extrapolated under imagined ideal conditions from the base principles of what is possible within the constraints of nature he observes. His thinking is that if some optimal outcome is even remotely attainable without defying any natural law, it should have already been accomplished long before he ever came along. To not already have the beautiful and orderly world he dreams of is a blight on the track record of every adult whose life has predated his arrival. They are the ones who should have already figured this out long ago.

Such is the burden of a mind that is inclined to see the logical outcome of things before it ever considers the real-world tactical changes that must be put into effect before that grand and shining outcome can ever be realized. It is a mind that lives in the plane of possibilities because that plane is so much neater and more efficient than the one that is slowed and diverted by mindless or incompatible human actions. And though there is a certain pure, unspoiled elegance to the mind that still sees the world for what it could, nay should be, with such childlike credulity, its direct application to reality as it is turns out to be rather limited.

Now begins the transition from a mentality where real strategy and real action were not necessary because utopia should have already been realized to one where the broken pieces that do not match the imagined ideal become the focus of an entire life. It is the discrepancy between the two that generates the great heroic ambition to change things and accomplish the wonders that reward someone with an incomparable sense of purpose. For if nothing ever needed improving, there could be no meaningful way to exist. That transition is a necessary part of growing up.

We will be very disappointed to realize for the first time that the world frequently does not work the way we intuitively envision that it should. It is because our minds are naturally attuned to possibility and solutions, while the world is much more predominantly oriented toward and by restraint. Most of those who came before us and exist concurrently with us are predisposed by their nature and their experiences to, on the whole, maintain systemic flaws the way they are. They have been, for better or worse, now at least partially defined by the cracks of their society and the evil its configuration invariably leads to. Our minds, by design, work very differently than those that accept the ugly world for how it is without ever considering how it could be otherwise. We begin at a state of perfect and heavenly operation and must work our way down to the dreary earthly reality.

As well, the unprincipled masses of underdeveloped humanity will, at practically every chance they are given, use our hopefulness and idealism as a means to take advantage of us. That is their predilection: Immediate personal gain, no matter the long-term or interpersonal costs. After once too often expecting people to be good and just and noble toward us merely because they state that it is their ambition to operate in such an elevated manner and then facing the sobering truth that they have used our idealist expectations to take something from us, we are likely to grow ashamed for the way we once looked upon our species with such hopefulness about its potential.

From here, it is a quick and thoughtless descent into the dark and embittered versions of us, and it is a long and dedicated task to pull ourselves out from that cave after we have entered. If we dwell there too long in our own resentment for the world failing to treat us fairly and live up to our noble standards for it, it becomes increasingly likely that we will never learn to manage and apply our darkness toward actual productive ends. We will end up accomplishing the very opposite of what we were destined to do with our natural temperaments, awareness, and abilities. We may even permanently condemn ourselves to live out our lives as the villainous versions of what we could and should have been. For this reason, heroic idealism is a precarious quality and one which every young adventurer must learn to place in its proper context against the backdrop of a world that will tear him apart for ever daring to dream of it.

Your amateur idealism is a profound gift because it gives you vision to move yourself and your world forward, but it will also certainly be a source of immense grief for you at times on the path. The trick, as it is with many things, lies in developing the insight, perspective, and discipline to recognize when the great discrepancy between your version of the optimal arrangement and the discouraging reality is one that can be logistically conquered, at least within the timeframe of your life or the period you are willing to devote to its realization. If you cannot do this, your complaints about the unpleasant world become just idle and undirected. You blame only a hazy conception of "society" for its failure to live up to the potential you have prescribed for it. But solutions to collective problems always begin with the individual, and the individual begins with you.

As you continue on your path, you must remember that your extreme difference in standards and expectations for this world is primarily due to the fact that this world was not made for you, and you were never meant for it. Yet, you cannot do anything about the fact that the only way for you to continue existing is to exist within it. There is simply nowhere else for you to go. And the only way for you to remain fulfilled and sane here is for you to acknowledge it as it is and commit to some kind of purposeful action here. It is only logical that the action you commit to will be directly related to the attainment of that ideal you perceive, in some small way at least. It will be something you can genuinely believe in, support wholeheartedly, and see at least a minor tangible amount of progress toward it as a direct consequence of your orderly intervention.

Aligning the practical with the theoretical in your mind is the first invisible but essential step toward the hero's endpoint of living as an embodiment of a set of ideals. Where normal minds operate according to an arbitrary and ever-changing set of exceptions and incidents that are primarily written by convenience and social expectation, the heroic life is the one that recognizes no difference between what is, in theory, an absolutism and eternally true and the dirty truth of life with its obstacles and barriers that make that absolutism inconvenient. But the temporary sacrifices that are required to remain an idealistic and absolutist person in a world that trails far behind are nothing compared to the sense of self-security that comes only from living up to the standards of your own idealism. In that way, your refusal to turn in your naiveté for the real world's realism is one of your greatest strengths. Maintain it, no matter the costs.

# 05
# Mindset and Strategy

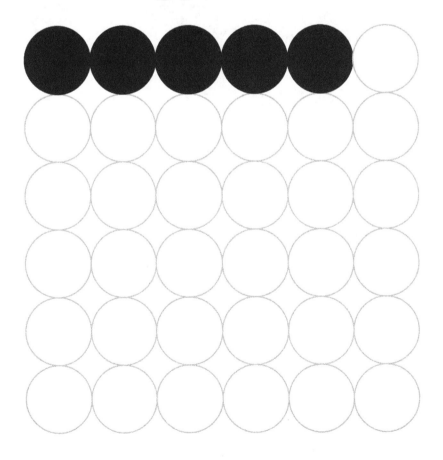

# Mindset and Strategy

*On the journey away from inherited ideas and toward authentic values, the heroic mind employs many frameworks to make sense of what it encounters. The mindsets we use in figuring the world out and our ideal roles within it determine everything we end up believing or doing. They show us how to find the hidden usefulness in even our most benign experiences and make meaning out of what, at first, seems to be meaningless. Unless we master how we think about our behavioral efficiency and the ways the world necessarily fits together, we delay the growth of our most important abilities.*

All power to alter reality derives from a person's interpretations of the concepts of purpose and meaning. What he finds meaningful depends on what appeals to his known priorities, which in turn depend on how he sees the workings of the world. The mind evaluates all experience as good or bad, relevant or irrelevant, or helpful or detrimental depending on its biases and goals. It easily forgets there are other ways to interpret things than how it initially does so. But to keep growing, it must remain open to watching and evaluating long after it might normally have stopped.

With time, such a mind relies evermore on familiar templates to organize the chaos of its unfamiliar observations. Minds need known structures to give order to experience so that they can separate what's useful from what's not. The right mindset enables the generation of meaning in revolutionary ways, even if it is just arranging old meaning differently than before. But if a person is not utterly mindful of how he organizes the many facets of his experience, his familiar categories will only lead him in circles or to permanent stagnation.

A self-aware thinker takes ownership of how he adds his cognition to reality. He knows he can decipher more meaning than if he were to remain a slave to known and former biases. He knows that he can mold all events into lessons pursuant to his goals. He can find the good in the horrendous. He can shape his perspective to assist him because he knows the state of his analysis. He is the master of his ideology, not a pawn of commonly accepted knowledge.

But to master the meaning one ascribes to reality is neither natural nor easy. Without defenses for assessing information, a mind loses control of its own paradigm. The stress of processing ideas incongruent with past assumptions grows heavy. Changes in observation come too quickly, and new data bombards the mind that is unready for it. Without attention to thought, a million outside forces may undermine the ability to draw new conclusions clearly. The power to strategize idiosyncratically is lost to the pressure of everyday thinking.

Our emotions are not random. At the root of every negative reaction, we hold a disappointed expectation. All our positive emotions stem from met desires. Our emotional health depends on the standards we set for how our lives should go. If we do not examine our standards, we prime ourselves for

25

long-term internal mental chaos. Without our critical self-examination of the associations we have adopted across our lives, our minds maintain their associations because to lose them feels like giving up a part of themselves.

Our minds build their paradigms to aid us, shaping the data they receive for this end as they perceive it. We get so good at this that we forget our mindsets are not inherent to reality. We impose our meaning on the truth because it helps us label new experience. But when reality won't align with our assumptions, our mindsets come to harm us. Our treasured memories, symbols, and associations, those footholds that bring us back to the moments that taught us how to interpret, must go, at least for a while. We must learn to see things more neutrally so we can replace our past associations with ones more useful to our present.

Most experience evacuates itself from mind just as soon as it enters. Relatively few memories are granted the privilege of living on as the reference points of the psyche. In a flash, our minds decide, often arbitrarily, what is suitable to keep for further application or study, and we hardly ever notice what they are up to. So, we must become uncommonly aware of what meaning we add to the world or what experiences we discard before considering their worth, or else the information retention strategies of our automated mindsets might hinder us from seeing what might be the most useful ways for us to be in the world.

Our specialization is our bias. If we attune our minds to better see some patterns, we turn them off from others. When we are accustomed to processing the same kinds of information into always similar arrangements, we begin to imagine all encounters as conforming to our mold. With predetermined filing, there is no space between what we experience and how we act on it. We have no chance to reflect on what is moral, true, or useful about our lives. We don't consider how we else we might respond. And so, we cease to grow.

Of course, some manner of framework will always be necessary in your cognition. A framework provides the boundary conditions for your mind to navigate its associations. It determines how you see your place in the world and the appropriate way to behave, which makes the world itself appear very different to you. Fortunately, however, when your mind's framework needs rearranging because it does not seem to serve you any longer, you can will yourself to see familiar concepts differently. You can watch for where your familiar eyes have added inappropriate meaning where it does not belong.

Altering your mindset alters the meaning of all you have observed. So long as your mind expects things to go a certain way, you stay locked into a spectrum of acceptable outcomes. Only by retaking control of your expectations can you engineer your future differently. Only then can you cease to be a slave to the past that you were handed. You'll be free to reinterpret your surroundings and find what else there is to gain from any situation.

So, question every thought or feeling that enters your awareness. This way, you can minimize the tampering of your mind upon reality. Whatever makes its way to your cognition, identify its origin. Whatever feelings present themselves, ask why they have the power to cause joy, terror, enthrallment, or devastation. There is always purpose to these emotions, but we often overlook it in the moment. We can neither use nor negate them if we do not understand them.

For an adaptable mind such as yours, there is no experience that cannot be interpreted to serve a purpose within its framework. Whatever may cause trauma or distress will lend you valuable insight if you are flexible enough to perceive it. When you can do this as you wish, you are no longer a victim of circumstance. Instead, you will be tapping into an endless supply of new data with which to make your own meaning and interpret your reality. And when the world stops telling you what you ought to want, you will be cast out, finally, on your own to discover it yourself.

# 06
# Insight and
# Innovation

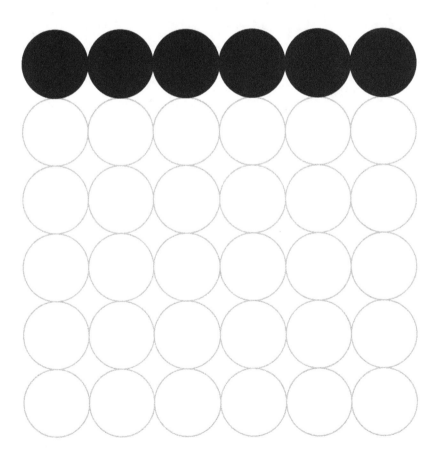

# Insight and Innovation

*To see the world's possibilities differently than the norm is an unavoidable blessing and a curse. Insight about such matters is a core part of what defines our unique roles in the world. It gives us novel options for considering the world itself beyond what others have settled into and pressure onto us. It makes us wholly responsible for determining what the right way for our lives to go will be because we are not so limited in the capacity to see. Infinite choice remains a present weight for us, and it may, ironically, stifle our ability to decide on even the most basic quandaries if we are not mindful.*

◆━━━━━━━━━━━━━●━━━━━━━━━━━◆

The uncommon mindset is a natural innovator of new solutions to old problems because it does not see them the same as other mindsets do. It even perceives the invisible issues that conventional personalities consistently overlook because they do not realize that something important requires changing and something urgent demands their attention. So, an insightful mind necessarily processes a higher amount or more complex arrangement of details. It never just sees what appears to be true. It sees what else must also be true to enable this apparent truth to persist. It sees what else can or will be true as a consequence and more, a thousand times over. And still, under the weight of all that noise, it must find a way to function and act usefully within the narrow space of what is acknowledged and shared as the only relevant reality.

When one ceases to accept on instinct the premise that the way things are seen or done is the way they must be done (or even the best way they could be done), the mind immediately opens to the infinite other avenues for arriving at the same or a superior conclusion that were always present but unnoticed by almost everyone. It is too much to take in, too much to manage for most, as it weighs painfully on the thoughts and emotions. It is so, so much easier to merely accept the common model for assessing reality's range of proper arrangements than to have to test them out oneself, disconnected from the carried-over models others use to simplify the process of figuring out how to act in every situation.

But the unseen cost of these savings in energy is the loss of the ability to think innovatively, to see the familiar world under all the different labels it could carry. In exchange for convenience and the nullification of pressing mental irritants, one can expect to sacrifice a great deal of their powers. They will diminish in their capacity to arrange the world in ways they are uniquely suited to their natures, for they will resign themselves to only following pathways already proven to work in mass application. They will forfeit the ability to forge their own means to a unique destiny all their own because it requires original perceptions and insights.

The primary disadvantage of life as a constant innovator of new channels around and through humanity's existing order is the incredible time and energy it demands of us merely to exist and to perceive reality, let alone to act upon those perceptions in calculated manners. Because it is in our nature to reason from first principles in almost every category and endeavor, it can

31

be tremendously difficult even to accept the conclusive methods ordinary people pass about for managing everyday tasks and burdens. Almost nothing is taken for granted in our exceptional perspective. Claims are not accepted at face value. Known truths require unpacking so that we may test them for efficiency and efficacy. We must always know why people are doing things the way they are before we can effectively imitate their behavior. This is a deeply frustrating way of living in the world, both for us and those who must put up with us.

Because it can be overwhelming to our minds to attempt to contemplate every potentially relevant detail about an action, a thing, or a strategy, the process is often paralyzing. It may very well make us seem utterly weak and feeble to ourselves and everyone we are unfortunate enough to be witnessed by whenever this occurs. Ironically, it is our great power that reduces us to this infantile state of powerlessness. All at once, the very worst aspects of us take over, and we must work at our capacity to try to steer ourselves back toward our better parts. But we cannot have the better without the worse, for they are logically necessary correlates.

The same qualities that make us superhuman when the stars align just so can turn us into subhumans when they are in any other arrangement not particularly suited to who we are. But what we should accept is that it is not us who are changing, only the contextual demands of what is happening all around us and the subjective values of the people whose opinions dominate the local cultural ecology. We remain the same and absolute. We cannot give up those traits that make us sometimes fragile without also removing our exceptional strength when circumstances suddenly change to require them. As well, we cannot expect ordinary minds to have the perspective to focus on the principle of who and what we are regardless of the moment. They are primed to see what is only right in front of them and affecting their emotions, not the timeless truths at play.

If you can apply your unique way of seeing things in the right measure and in the right situation, it will be received with the sense of impossible awe that it warrants. Through the impact of your insight, minds that could not otherwise have hoped to crawl out of their own confines begin to get a hint of the broader principles at play in their familiar situations, and so the once-inconceivable becomes attainable to everyone. Options in every domain begin to extend far beyond what is currently practiced into the new, vaster realm of what could possibly be done once you ignore comfort and common habit.

Wisdom, which is, in actuality, just clear vision not bogged down by incidentally accumulated bias from personal experience, can be a superpower to many. It usually comes to you through broad sets of experience that make principle apparent and enables you to think beyond the boundaries of what you happened to have been through. It is a far greater gift and more capable tool than specialty in any specific area of study, for that specificity also becomes a limitation to perspective. It is what enables you to live beyond your own knowledge and offer insight even to experts who cannot seem to think their way around a configuration of confounding problems because they lack the training they would need to do so.

32

Your overhead perspective does come from training or memorized instruction. It is the product of the ability to piece reality together even when no one tells you how you ought to do so. It makes you immensely valuable to the world whenever the world cannot see how its own habits are harming it and holding it back from what it could accomplish. For this reason, your priority is to practice and learn to control and present your gift in ways that matter, as that is how you will innovate a better path for the world to gradually move upon. You lay the track that others shall one day follow, and you nestle more authentically into your own as you meander.

# 07
# Emotion and Conviction

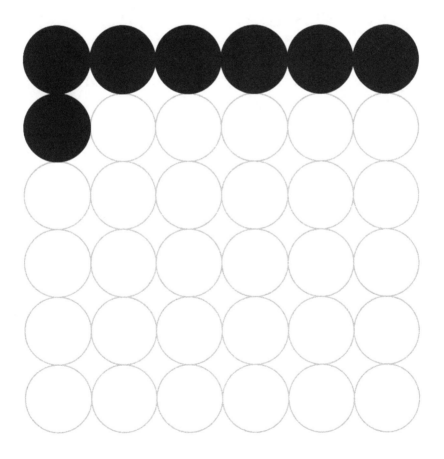

# Emotion and Conviction

*The ability to feel a complex range of emotions is a major aspect of humanity's signature power. Each emotion serves a function, but the feeler does not always appreciate its role. And so, it is common to treat our feelings as obstacles to our desires, not as the mechanisms that will help acquire them. We believe that we should seek to rise above emotional influence, but how we react with our emotions is a distinct part of who we are. How we embrace or reject our feelings determines, in large part, the paths our lives will take. Our strength comes from conviction when we capitalize on the flow of our emotions.*

Most people, over time, come to willingly embody only a minor portion of their range to feel. And by detaching themselves from their strongest feelings, they eliminate their own capacity to act with conviction upon them. They fall into patterns of solely convenient action because they only ever feel convenient emotions, meaning those that are tolerated within their microsocial environments or which they have arbitrarily come to see as a valid part of their personality. Whatever overwhelming emotions they can still experience, which should be treasured tools, become constraints to their expression.

An emotion, at the peak of its intensity, colors its host's experience and provokes a particular style of expression. Each has circumstantial utility, helping in some situations and hindering in others. Emotional tools may show up as sadness, greed, excitement, fear, or any other impulse to incentivize behavior in the subjective perspective of the feeler. Emotion often subjugates agency, so the feeler can no longer think about what he should actually be doing according to the standards set by his conscious values. Strong feelings have done the deciding for him. The tool is now the master, and the tail wags the dog.

Within the confines of a society, however a person is primarily impressed upon to express his emotions by his peers and overseers sets the template for how he feels them. Social authorities establish the limits to his expression before he is even capable of recognizing them. The more powerful his native expressions, the more the minds of society will seek to cage him. But emotions are primordial functions that are antecedent to human opinion about them, as those judgments themselves are just emotional responses to the concept of emotion. Reducing them to conform with fleeting social custom also necessarily reduces the power and conviction of the one who feels them.

The role of feelings is to discriminate subjective bad from good in the world. These evaluations shape one's reactions to every experience, aiding or opposing the ability to reason well about what's going on. Emotion only becomes the enemy of intellect if one should refuse to think about the ways one feels. In an optimal organism, the thinking brain strategizes to acquire what the feeling mind desires, and those subjective desires align with what is demonstrable as an objective moral good. This is the only way to avoid going to war with either oneself or reality.

When we interfere with the trajectory of an emotion, we sabotage the balance it would bring to us by satisfying the want that it signals. But we will continue to shun our emotions if they, in our limited perspective, lack a clear and instant function. We come to see some feelings as invaders that keep us from being our ideal selves and living within the limited range of expression we consider healthy and valid. We deny our unwelcome emotions, and so we forsake the benefits they are meant to carry. Because we favor only the emotions we are comfortable with, we apply the wrong feelings in the wrong situations, in the long run creating greater conflict than we resolve.

Happiness, by default, becomes the ideal state that we are always chasing after, and anything lesser is scarcely permitted to remain. However, the spoils of happiness are never stable. If we should ever commit the error of chasing only joy, we will go to war with the rest of the spectrum of experience. Happiness comes only in the moments we want for nothing more than what we have. It is an idle state where we can do virtually nothing to interrupt the contentment of the moment or lose what we have earned. Our capacity to act is functionally disabled. Happiness is our reward for correct action, not our default state.

Emotions, mismanaged, corral our attention into wild directions. They make us act what we perceive as uncharacteristically, but that is only because we have a limited definition for our character. So long as our emotions remain in their wild and unpredictable state, we are fortresses set against ourselves, unable to act on our powerful but latent potential. We may resort to anger uncalled for if it seems the quickest path to impact. Anger instigates meaningful action but, as well, carries collateral disruption. Sadness is the process of reflection, which we need in order to improve our own behavior. But if sorrow overstays, it defeats our motivation. Our suffering is essential to our growth. We must be willing to endure pain to accomplish what we care about.

Should emotions persist beyond their necessity, judgment becomes cloudy. We respond more and more to our emotional projections of what is happening and not to what is real. Caught in looping emotions, we are not the masters of our own lives any longer. We are slaves to automatic signals, simpler creatures who hold no self-reflection. And emotion, like illness, can be wildly contagious. Possessed by feelings, we cannot help but spread them to those who are amenable to our influence. Only deliberate emotional fortitude can halt the malady from spreading, and choice begins with conscious self-awareness of the state we have fallen into.

When you observe that some emotions recur too often or stick around too long, analyze and try to see them as nothing more than holdovers of a once-conditioned version of you. New responsibilities require you to abandon ancient patterns. If your emotions still flare up where they should not, resist the urge to correct or overcompensate with active denial. Instead, gain some distance from yourself for a time. From a far-off point of view, you can assess more clearly why you feel as you do.

With experience, you will discover that negative emotions are just as useful as their positive extremes. Sorrow is recalled more easily than joy, and injury generates the incentive to improve. No pain ever has to turn you cruel or dull your sensibility if you learn how to process it. Pain can make you kind, so you will seek to spare others the injuries that even you have only just survived. Your pain reminds you how it feels to push harder than you knew you could and grow to more than yesterday. In many ways, it sits at the core of your conviction.

Works of art, in all their forms, offer packaged emotional states you may not normally experience and encapsulated empathy. They foster specific feelings in their consumers. Art can supplement what your constraining life has lacked. Through art's controlled scenarios, you can practice every emotion and grow adept in them, eventually coming to fully realize your humanity with them, supplementing your growth with curated experiences you would not otherwise encounter.

Whatever your feelings, know they will pass if you allow them the opportunity. The universe will reshuffle itself, and your mind will adjust with it. Add no resistance, and the storm moves through you having met its purpose of altering your behavior or affecting your imbalance. So, appreciate the empty peace that follows. Peace is the product of total self-expression. Mold your reactions to your terrain, and your emotions will remain allies to rely on, not distractions from your values.

# 08
# Faculties and Strengths

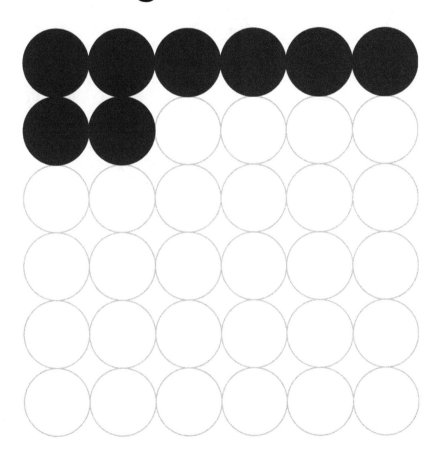

# Faculties and Strengths

*Raw ability matters greatly on the path to self-development because it represents the furthest possible end of an uncommon person's inherent power to affect reality. We must learn never to conceal what we can do. We must never lessen ourselves for the sake of the comfort of peers if we are to progress against stagnation, which is our destined role in the world. Our minds and bodies are laboratories to discover novel functions and things we can do that others cannot within the domains of existing that come most naturally to us.*

Every gifted person, at some point in his development, might lament that he may never be the absolute best at any skill that he pursues. This competitive mentality, inherited from an uninspired society and ignorant of the value of a natural diversity of strengths, has robbed him of his individuality. It has pushed him to exist as the byproduct of a series of inane comparisons to people who do not deserve a say in his development. So, he has lost sight of the depth of his potential. His self-analysis occurs through only the perspective of his social utility.

It is, of course, only natural to seek uniqueness amongst one's peers, for each person to want to stand apart from the common features of their tribes. Individuals wish to be seen as shining and irreplaceable in some regard, but many of the ways they pursue individuality are fleeting. They focus on those categories of behavior most visible to ordinary eyes. They rely on the context of what is normal to determine how they might be considered different from the norm. Their development becomes entangled because they care about comparison to their peers.

To be exceptional is to be set apart from the local norm in important ways by one's inescapable design. A naturally great painter understands the symbolic concepts of color and proportion as they relate to visual perception. A musician's ears are made to detail changes in the relationship among sounds better and his mind to rearrange it as he pleases. An architect must hold the faculty to see the ways his creations hold together in an ongoing dance of function and form.

A person's specializations, including all their possible applications, may not be apparent right away, and this may contribute to their frustration with the course of their own lives. Natural abilities may remain hidden until their owner develops the eyes to see them. In fact, what have seemed like burdens for most of life may, in fact, be the embryos of strengths one was not ready to realize. His early social environment did not allow him to. So now, he can only begin to learn his potential by abandoning former social context.

Furthermore, it is a mistake to believe that being naturally adept in any manner should make life easy for the gifted mind. Many things commonly considered easy feel foreign to a mind built in an uncommon way. Aptitude is not a linear pursuit. Some faculties help only to a point. Others are wholly detrimental in all but a rare situation. What is a blessing in one context may be terminal in some other. An outlier among humanity must assess how his faculties can be arranged to harm or help him.

Absent our critical analysis, we never recognize our faculties for what they could become. We may overlook any of an infinite number of possible applications that circumstance has not forced out of us. But by studying the principles from which our sets of skill derive, we come to see that no power is ever the result of one faculty operating in isolation from the rest. There are many things at work in us to produce the traits we favor. Their interactions can be pulled apart and rearranged into a greater number of ways than we could ever explore. The process of self-uncovering is never truly complete.

Though the world trains us to admire people who seek excellence in a solitary quantifiable way, no strength is ever limited to a single application. Society cares only for what it can measure and repurpose, but the exceptional mind sees past the limits of this trap. It combines the many facets of its personality into unprecedented solutions, never relying on a single learned asset or behavior for its primary definition. This is the ongoing strategy of an adaptable life that never stops remaking itself and growing.

Our minds require context for their thoughts and feelings to be useful. They create meaningful space for their uncommon parts to belong, reshaping their world in the process. But they cannot do this so long as their most potent abilities hide beneath a young lifetime of inhibitions. Each of us must grow willing to step away from common competition. We must accept the fact that our designs are not compatible with social superiority contests. Our power is not so simple as that. The burden is ours to find the environments that will activate our advantages and offer heroic rewards.

You will recognize your strengths when you can produce great results without equivalent effort. When ordinary minds are stifled, you will press on without exhaustion. You arrive at answers without heavy strain upon your thinking. You know what to do sans deliberation in some categories of experience when others are always unsure of themselves. You can visualize the outcomes you desire, and your body conforms to create them. Your natural faculties won't fail when conditions are suboptimal. When your environment falls into disrepair and disorder is all around you, you will still act. You will remain operational when others become taxed to exhaustion. These are your natural faculties. Get to know them, for they will form the means to every great action. Your lifelong struggle is to learn to apply your strengths for the purposes deemed worthy by your values.

When you follow your curiosity and experiment with how to apply your strengths, there is no end to who you may become. You cannot predict all the things you may go on to accomplish. When you aren't acting to fit in any longer, you do only what works by your own standards of success. You become malleable without the pressure to conform. Once you identify a category, principle, or activity for which your interest remains ongoing and stable, you will know where to focus your development.

Arranged in complementary manners, uncommon characteristics morph into potent abilities. Sooner or later, their impact cannot be ignored by you or the world around you. You only need the patience to see your unspoken faculties develop into tangible and effective new abilities. If you begin your life at a seeming disadvantage to your peers because your strengths are not right away obvious, you may still go on to outpace them once your many hidden faculties come about from within you.

Work now to cultivate a diversity of traits, even though they may have no obvious implementation. Never let yourself believe that you must specialize too narrowly or at once devote yourself to a predetermined plan. Adopt learning as a habit for the sake of itself because you know you can't predict all the categories of knowledge or ability that will be useful throughout your life. Focus on the spaces between common categories. In them, you will find a deep and adaptable source of novel strengths. Far beyond the areas where others have established their common value judgments, you will find many talents for which the world knows no context. It is your lifetime destiny to give them that new context.

# 09
# Boundary and Error

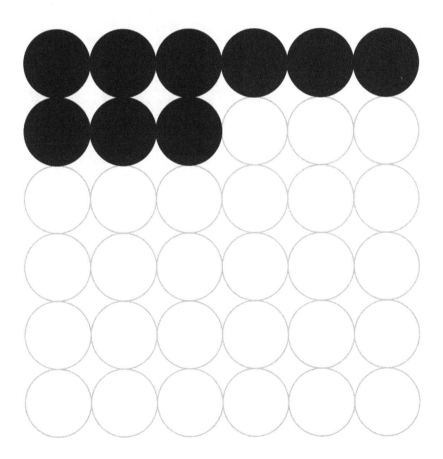

# Boundary and Error

*A heroic person cannot rest for very long within the boundaries of known comfort and abilities. It is in our nature to test ourselves daily, in every way we can, until we conquer any restraints that keep us from achieving what we fundamentally desire. We learn from the injuries we sustain and the strain of great effort that, left unchecked, our inescapable deficiencies might misalign us with our values, leaving us unable to focus where we ought to. So, we design our lives to negate our failings, even converting them to assets if we are able.*

To be an outlier carries responsibilities and burdens. There will be ordinary things that hinder unconventional thinkers inordinate amounts. Those who process differently won't always have the luxury of enjoying the same simple pleasures as everyone else. Physically, there will be feats they cannot conquer, even when their peers insist such feats are easy. Some experiences will hurt, even when the general consensus is that they should not. The outlier will start to think this means there is something wrong with him for failing to meet the competency standards set by social norms.

Despite their strengths, which are usually obvious, none, even the most gifted people, can pretend to be strong or invincible forever. Sooner or later, they meet their impassable barriers. The gifted will check such barriers, not at first accepting them as absolutes. They already know through their experience how easily some obstacles can be broken or bypassed once they muster the skill and effort to. But some barriers, they will realize, are built into the unchangeable fabric of the universe. There will never be anything they can do or become to undermine them any more than they can undermine reality herself.

A person who lacks a hero's resilience will turn away from difficulty as soon as it arises. Only a heroic mindset allows for the realization that what is, at first, a challenge might be overcome through a change in one's approach. But an ordinary person avoids the discomfort of performing poorly in his own eyes or society's. He is afraid to become the fool and contradict the social narrative he presents about his role in the world. That shame prevents him from converting his many weaknesses into strengths. He is not willing to been seen as fragile for even a time. He has carved out a narrow place for himself where he can be at peace in his society.

On the other hand, the exceptional mind knows feebleness is inevitable every time it begins exploration of a new domain. The pain of confronting what seems to be an unscalable weakness is necessary for its maturation. In challenging personal deficiency, it learns beyond doubt which aspects of itself can be relied on. Then, its confidence is truly earned, which makes it more capable than any mind that is naturally strong in any specific area and never learns from the perspective of the opposite.

We who have still never seen the impact of our failings may never start to realize we even have them. So, under blind ignorance of our own limitations, we never learn to manage them. But the further we stray from the sheltered conditions under which our lives began, the more we will be forced to confront the effects of our own shortcomings.

If we have been reared in comfort and privilege, we have almost certainly never received the negative feedback necessary to deter us from persisting in mistakes. Because we have known only strength and good fortune, we may have never felt the pull to improve, as people plagued by weakness often do. We, the strong, take our strength for granted, so our progress is in danger of ending up prematurely capped by our designs. We may face no significant challenges through which to suffer and grow, no stabbing pains to alleviate, and the trauma we are missing might be our biggest source of growth.

The first time we step away from early comfort, we realize we lack the tools to process the sudden exposure to a greater proportion of reality's chaos. Because we have always been assisted in exploration, experiencing life without a narrative or plan reveals pieces of self that convenience may have not yet revealed. This leads to greater understanding of the nature of our weaknesses, which might, in time, give us the confidence to master them. This is the first step to a state where our weaknesses truly do not matter.

As it is with strength, context is what gives power and meaning to weakness. There is always only a narrow window of relevance through which we evaluate our failings. We all have inabilities that aren't relevant to how we live or the goals that we pursue. None of us know everything there is to know within any given domain of study. No one can accomplish the physically impossible. Ordinarily, we neither notice nor care. Only the pain of an unmet expectation draws our attention to the ability or knowledge we are lacking. This pain grants us the incentive to improve ourselves.

When a weakness recurs, determination is required to investigate its origins. What does the limitation represent? What wants or needs is it preventing us from acquiring? Many of the things we tell ourselves we ought to care about are only remnants of old paradigms we have yet to put behind us. We waste our attention on shortcomings that shouldn't matter in the context of our goals. We must be focused enough to narrow our attention to what we have decided is eternally important.

Always remember that your story is one of overcoming limitations. The more you come to know yourself, the more you will lust to embody your strengths free of the obstacles of conventional obligations. So, you must foresee where your natural weaknesses might prevent you from acquiring your desires. All other limitations can be safely ignored. All other judgments are moot. Anything that does not inhibit the pursuit of your highest values is not worthy of your concern.

Fundamental to your continued growth is acceptance of the premise that there are more sides to you than you will ever know in the limited span of your lifetime. Not all parts of you will be apparent right away. Anguish, like a spotlight, calls your attention to behaviors routinely ignored because they seemed too inconvenient to address. A growth-oriented mind like yours places its attention where it sees it is needed for development to happen. Awareness of your weaknesses will give you a type of self-knowledge that ordinary minds can never know.

Begin with a clear understanding of the distance between where you are and where you know you would like to be. With perspective of this gap, you can reverse engineer the means to traverse it. Examine the patterns of thought and action embodied by the people who can do what you desire. Begin then to inwardly map their behavior onto your own mind and body so you can identify the rules that govern their behavior. These are principles you can adopt, so long as you are not totally identified with your present limitations.

Keep your deficiencies close to your heart, for that is the only way to start to obviate your failings. Test every limit so you can see how much they actually matter. Focus your attention on amending the limitations that prevent you from getting what you want from life. Willpower, adaptation, and analysis can all make up for whatever is lacking in natural faculty. Don't assume your shortcomings in any random contextual domain must define you in any meaningful sense or affect the whole of your cognition.

# 10
# Interest and Curiosity

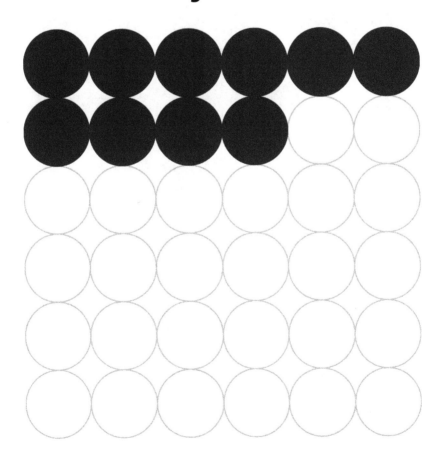

# Interest and Curiosity

*Change is inevitable, but a hero only welcomes change when he is curious about what the unknown will bring to his attention. It should be our consistent characteristic to seek new challenges that pique our interest, engage our emotions, and enliven our passions. Otherwise, we risk repeating only the same familiar patterns all our lives. Ideal curiosity strikes a balance between perpetual novelty and stagnant structure. It enables us to exert some level of control over the changes we must endure so that we evolve according to the orderly patterns of our own nature and not the randomness of a world not guided by principle.*

Reality is always moving, evolving, and redefining herself. Each person in reality is likewise in motion. An open mind always lusts for more than what it knows. Things unfamiliar, perhaps at first intimidating, welcome the exploration of their mysteries. Ordinarily, people reach the peak of their ability to pursue new knowledge just shortly after physical maturity. Then begins the prolonged march of mental decline. Thoughts grow uniform and repeated. Expansion all but ceases. It is the trajectory of every psyche.

Decay, though at some point inevitable, can be delayed for a long while by a mind's strong desire for novelty. Nurturing the mind's natural curiosity slows its long descent into chaos. Novelty brings traction and prolongs the rising time of consciousness. If a person should indulge in the chase of things that inspire him, his curiosity will lift his development past normal human capacity.

It hardly matters, at the first steps, what inspires the exceptional heart to beat or the mind to willingly stretch itself. It only matters that there are enough experiences to challenge the way things have been so far. Following the curious impulse, even as random acts of creative inspiration, opens pathways to new levels of operation and higher orders of willpower. A curious explorer quickly learns that there are worlds within him that are as vast as the great unknown universe all around him.

Curiosity leads explorers into areas of reality they could not imagine, horrors and wonders beyond their present understanding. If the world appears uninteresting, it is because the observer has limited his field of vision to perspectives where only uninteresting things can occur. Curiosity can move a person beyond his ways of living and thinking. It can delay his descent into the stillness of dying. Curiosity is even vital for interpersonal intimacy, as it is the prime mover in wanting to get to know another person more deeply and include another identity as a part of one's own.

Curiosity has the power to turn offending agents into tools for creation. A curious mind does not close itself to what it does not instantly favor. People only become close-minded once they are no longer curious about what they do not understand. Bigotry is born when diversity is no longer intriguing but instead conjures defenses that halt emerging opportunities. The curious mind does not turn away from these ugly feelings; it seeks to know them in and out. The desire to always know more of reality can overcome any emotional traps on the path to emancipation.

From the time we are born, we are privy to boundaries set by the people who came before, just as they themselves were bounded by the ones who arrived even earlier. Though it is natural to want protect the young from the detriments of early exploration. Wherever there is something to discover, there comes with it the possibility of harm. There is unavoidable risk to exploration.

As we cross into the unknown, we may not like what we encounter on the other side of change. Our fear balances that impulse to explore the wild unknown with necessary apprehension. Hesitation prevents us from departing before we're ready. Fear is a cautious response to what the mind might not be ready to categorize. With familiarity, fear evaporates. With understanding, control returns.

By the time we reach adulthood, the curiosity we knew as children may likely have dissipated. Each day becomes then a battle against the failing of our interest. Our aged minds must question every limit they were given and, if necessary, reset their boundaries before losing their inertia. Our limits will then come to be only those we rediscover through our own decisions.

To fearful minds, curiosity is a danger. It seems insatiable if we are unwilling to follow where it leads. Curiosity raises questions uncomfortable to answer. It pulls at something we cannot ever really reach. If we cannot harness curiosity's motion, we may see it as a threat to our stability. Our lives will become stagnant compared to those who ride their curiosity into bolder pursuits each day. And if we cannot make it across our fear of the unknown, we will never receive the rewards of exploration.

Our parents and other protective figures shielded us too much from what we, in our infancy, could not even know to be afraid of. We have lived under the shadows of their limits so long that we do not know the real limits from the imagined ones. It is up to us alone to find the right balance between the safety of what we know and the expansion into what we do not.

Age is a cruel and inescapable tyrant. You will, one day, lack the energy to explore reality so fearlessly as you do now. Your activities will grow limited as time moves forth and entropy invades. The aged mind gets fooled into believing it has learned all it ever needs to.

While indulging curiosity is essential, you cannot be so reckless as to follow every whim however you like. Many sacrifices are too great to justify or bear. Not everything lost can be recovered. Injuries never fully heal. With maturity, you will continue to explore new territory in ways less arbitrary than you did before. There will be a persistent method to your adventures. Even when curiosity leads into unhappiness, following it further will be the only way out. Curiosity will, sooner or later, lead you where you ought to be.

Because your time and your energy will always be finite, you must rationally select how to apply your curiosity. You must know yourself well enough to know what you care about and devote your attention to. You cannot be all things in life and explore all areas, no matter your potential. The best you can do is to always be challenging your knowledge of who you are and how you ought to act but not chaotically so. Make yourself uncomfortable but always with a strategy and a purpose.

Narrowing your focus should never be a compromise of your values or a sacrifice of your ambition. Each day, you can challenge your paradigm in countless simple ways. You can change whatever seems ordinary into something exceptional. The passions you have known since childhood can be expressed through a million outlets. You never shut yourself off from new information but grow more selective about what information to pursue.

Infuse your life with the principles of growth now, before curiosity becomes a chore. Push against its dying whenever it dwindles. Expansion must become as natural to you as the act of breathing, a fundamental part of your existence as a self-aware human being inhabiting the body that you do. If you keep your heart and your mind open to all that is difficult and terrifying, discomfort will become a dear mentor to you. You will seek it out because comfort has nothing left to teach you.

# 11
## Challenge and Trial

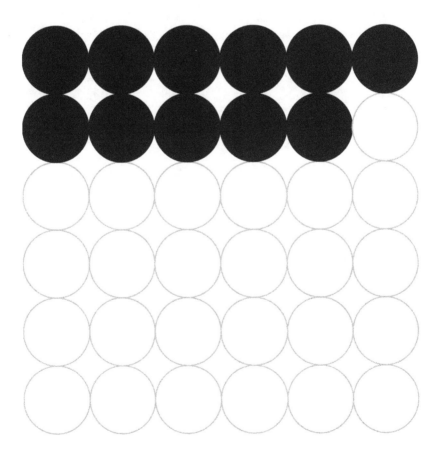

# Challenge and Trial

*A hero only truly tests himself in crisis. It is only when everything is working against us and we persevere against discomfort that our conviction rightfully strengthens. Only then do we know ourselves to be worthy of our own standards. On the quest for the permanent growth of character, we learn, beyond doubt, where our ideals falter or prevail against endless waves of challenge. So long as the path remains easy, our actions are not choices, and we are not becoming more of ourselves than we were when we started.*

◆———————————◆———————————◆

Without warning, any aspect of the reality one knows may rid itself of the patterns one expects of it. In these moments, the intentional actor must be strong enough to adapt his behavior, so he can maintain his life's familiar order. When reality suddenly demands something new from him, the novelty of unexpected change may stifle his behavior. His mind will be thrown into turmoil until he surpasses the trial he is facing.

A person who has never endured through troubling changes cannot know with any certainty that he holds the will to act how he knows is right no matter the challenges he faces. His assumed moral dedication is only a series of stories about a human life he calls his own. His abilities exist only in the situations he has established for himself. He must surpass trials tailored to his identity to know it is really his own.

The capacity for great vision also creates the propensity to waste through life in idle daydreams. A dreamer only philosophizes about who he might become under more ideal conditions. He prefers his imaginary self-image to the disappointing reality. Rarely do the dreamers ever act upon their claims to who they are. Rarely do they venture away from their acquired comforts, only projecting from a place of total safety.

But for existential development to continue, it is sooner or later necessary to move past the conceptual and embody all theoretical beliefs as actions. A person must apply his principles to all of reality's shared spaces. Whatever begins as an idea must actualize in his behavior. The more he can test his values against the conditions of his environment, the more he will transform reality to be more aligned with them.

It's easy to forget that every part of our present understanding of reality began as foreign information. It was not always present or necessary to our function. The world gave us countless rules and parameters before we even knew we could reject them. That is why we don't know who we are or our place within the world. We don't know how we really ought to act because we have so little real experience to draw from. We do not know the world as it really is.

With heightened awareness may come hesitation about how to act in rather ordinary situations. The exceptional mind sees countless layers of nuance and causality that influence its judgment. So long as we feel unprepared to process whatever intimidating things we encounter, we cannot embody our values. As such, we must integrate, consciously and unconsciously, the things that define us before our success in an unpredictable time ever depends on it.

Most of us have never known what a world working against us really looks like. That is why we do not know, beyond doubt, where our convictions will falter under stress. We've grown comfortable and arrogant in projection. That's why we still question just who we really are. Without a test to prove it, we cannot rely on our ideas about our values.

It is almost always easier to stick with what we know, no matter how much we despise it, than to change our behavior and begin to act in novel ways. This is because any new knowledge and ideals must first endure the doorway of the conscious mind before the unconscious can adopt them. When an idea is still foreign, we must hold it always in mind, and there will always be some delay or inefficiency if we must think before we act. Once fully integrated, however, knowledge operates independently in our bodies.

We often hesitate to act on new ideas because we aren't certain about what we think we care about. We lack complete acceptance of the values we say define us at our cores. Until it has made the transition to our intuition, new information requires major effort for us to implement. There is friction to the process, which makes for unavoidable delays and inefficiencies. Unconscious action comes to us through practice and certainty. In certainty, we can do what we know is right without deliberation because we have accepted the truth on every level.

All your strengths, values, and convictions are worthless without your actions to support them. When come the times that your choices are the deciding factor for important matters, your task is to evaluate extraordinary situations without fear so that you can act rightly under pressure. If you lose your mind in the overwhelm of a foreign situation when your action would be the factor that turns a situation toward order, you will fail to uphold your sacred values.

On the screen of your imagination, you can simulate extreme circumstances before they occur. You can imitate experiential data in your mind, testing where your convictions hold or falter under uncertain circumstances. You can envision complex, sensory-heavy scenarios yet to happen that will drive your development past your present limitations.

On your quest for growth, allow some tailored chaos to flood your perception for a time. Let it play out as realistically as possible, and monitor how you respond. Suspend your disbelief of this fantasy long enough to feel as though these imagined tests were really happening. Practice how you wish to be able to respond when intimidation overtakes you. These experiments will make real, lasting changes to your psychological self. What you do when real life is on the line will now be different. Through repeated, imaginary exposure, the novelty of an experience will pass. The unpredictable impact on your emotions will be nullified by self-imposed familiarity. When a strange new emergency arises, you will perceive it as somehow manageable and familiar, despite its foreign clothing.

Major physical changes come about as the product of lifetimes of internal evolution. So work now to equip your body and mind to act rightfully, without hesitation, when rightful action without hesitation is required in the world. Eventually, your outlying behavior will offer a new standard for select individuals who need a powerful example to reach for.

When you are confident in the values of your identity, you will march headstrong into stressful situations. You will take on challenges that make others run. You will not back down when ordinary people cower. Whether you succeed or fail in any given trial, your intervention will lead to an elevation of your ability to operate in the world and a sense of purpose in your life. When you are ready, you will act in the way that you must simply because you must, and you will do so without shame or hesitation.

# 12
# Ability and Practice

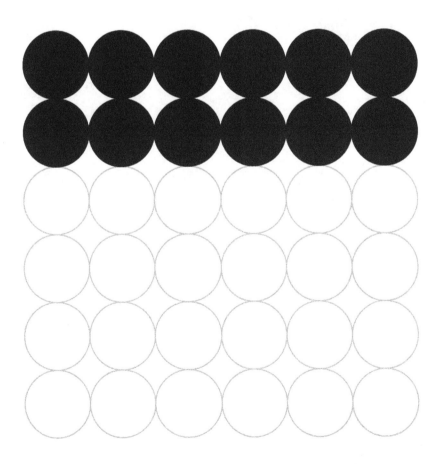

# Ability and Practice

*A person of heroic character, foregoing social norms, has entered a lifelong commitment with growth. We can never be totally satisfied with what we know and can offer. We remain addicts for expansion, for it is the only way we know to avoid our imminent self-destruction. Our natural state is not sufficient to embody our ideals, so our faculties must be developed and renewed through constant application, forever working just slightly beyond our comfortable boundaries.*

It is impossible for even the most gifted person to be productive without a sense of purpose to give context to his actions. Without an understanding of what he is trying to accomplish and why, he will be lost from the outset of any quest. He will only make progress for the sake of progress, growing wildly in any direction that is both measurable and socially condoned.

All actions become part of their enactors' recurring experience of themselves. The body forms itself around what its behavior teaches it that it is necessary for it to learn. So, as early as he can, the actor should develop the discipline to focus the development of new abilities upon only activities that serve his genuine values.

The world, however, elects its champions for their singular accomplishments in isolated fields. People do not receive recognition for abilities that do not contribute to social importance. Only big events are noteworthy to society's limited mindset. But real worth is not dependent on an outcome or a metric. It is built from many layers of nuance and is not always obvious.

When a person starts a new endeavor, his understanding is limited by what he believes he already knows. He explores every possible outcome within the confines of the space that is familiar. But this is only the beginning. Every observation reveals more of what there is to still observe. Once beyond the threshold of the familiar, his task is to take in what his mind and body are prepared to process and make it useful. The more of any domain he masters, the more he becomes prepared to notice. Gradually, reality unfolds herself to him.

Our journey to discover who we are and embody what we care about will almost always be overlooked by our peers. They will not be aware of what our experiences mean to us. When we spend our time in ways that do not conform to prevailing social narratives, society will make it hard for us to continue unabated. It may tell us we are wasting our lives pursuing what it presumes to be the wrong activities. It ignores the unlimited arrangements a human life might take when left to follow its own interests in whatever manner it desires.

To develop new abilities, our time must be always spent in line with what we value. The more consciously we control our time, the better we will convert experience to ability. Interest brings engagement to our actions, so, despite the expectations of the ordinary, we must always be acting upon whatever carries our highest degree of interest. Without interest, experience passes out of mind and never accumulates. Moments carry on with no trace of influence. All our mindless moments are lost forever.

To be meaningful, our development must not be bound to society's favored pastimes, and we must realize that any time invested in things we care about is never wasted. All activities that engage the body, intellect, or emotions contribute to our development.

What might seem on the surface to be superficial pastimes can have lasting impacts on the structures of our minds. Importance in the eyes of our society does not matter.

But the societal mind rushes to fill any spaces it identifies. It thinks giving something its attention makes it meaningful. It receives validation in its cares every time it recruits new adherents to its rituals. To maintain our focus on the things we know we care about, we must not let the world hijack us with its pressure to conform to other matters.

Your being is a tool that must be honed to be useful, but only you can know what to hone within the context of your values. When you are firm in your ideals, you can shape your mind and body to uphold them.

The development of new skill requires you to transpose information across many foreign domains into the unique architecture of your mind. Few are the teachers qualified to present important information in forms appropriate for your specialized mind. You become your own tutor when you encounter something that provokes your interest, and it is you who challenges yourself to deconstruct its workings. Through this exploration, you will come to know your mind's ideal way of learning.

Do not quickly fall into despair because you cannot see how your present abilities contribute to your passions. Your diversity of traits, once nurtured, will birth emergent qualities. When all your faculties convert seamlessly to actions, you will do things you never imagined. You will do things no one who knows you can even predict or imitate. So, do not sacrifice your nuance for minds that judge too quickly and forget just as soon. Their approval is fleeting, and by them you will never be celebrated for authenticity.

Proficiency appears in many forms, all of which can be combined into unlimited arrangements. A mind unimpeded by the world's stagnant categories creates connections others overlook. Your existence will only be made useful to reality through your arrangement of learned abilities, not merely one or two in obvious concentrations. You could spend the rest of your life rearranging only what you already know about yourself into countless manifestations of the same basic competencies and still never run out of things to do.

Never accept that the way people have organized their competencies is the way they must be organized. Focus your development on what will resolve the struggles that break the order of your reality. Train your body in the motions to arrange reality as you desire. Sacrifice the unnecessary categorical models at play in your society. Discipline yourself to devote your attention to activities that transform you into a greater embodiment of your values.

# 13
# Foolery and Preparation

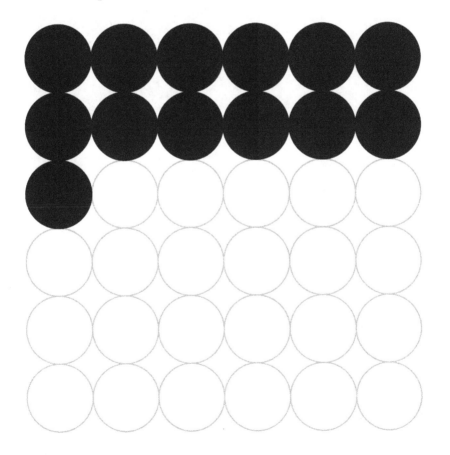

# Foolery and Preparation

*A meaningful and effective life requires leisure in proportion to the damage it inflicts through its countless trials against the hero's enduring psyche. Recreation helps our minds recover from their stresses so that they can tackle whatever next they face. Downtime creates the space to reconsider how well our chosen courses align with the principles of who we are discovering ourselves to be and, if necessary, alter the paths we follow. Recreational indulgences grant the opportunity to practice new skills and knowledge before they come to matter in actual trials.*

Identity development is the process of accumulating complementary parts into a new and integrated whole. The structure of a life only and necessarily expands when it is ready to, building atop what it has expanded into already. Its evolution is never the total reworking of one thing into another nor the complete wiping away of the past that led into the present. The person who needlessly splits life into independent factions ceases to be whole. If he believes his future is separate from his past, he becomes a partial and divided person, cut off at the legs from his formation.

On the path toward maturity, there will be changes that manifest too quickly for any mind to integrate. So, lives are frequently thrust into chaos during the most vulnerable stages of their development. Too much of this chaos accumulated at one time threatens to derail hard-won development before it has been able to settle. So, by evolutionary necessity, there is a natural buffer to this chaos. Neoteny and childish traits, the type adults are so often eager to distance their present social identities from, protect the mind from the harmful effects of its own hurried evolution. Remaining somewhat playful throughout life allows a mind to adapt more fluidly when it really needs to.

For this reason, among many others, the time a person has in youth is an irreplaceable gift. Conditions are optimal when young to prepare for the trials of maturity. If a person should rush through the preparatory stages of life, he will not learn the lessons required for his ongoing survival. He will not gain the abilities imperative for adapting to ever-changing challenges and fulfillment.

When young, people unconsciously prepare for all the ways they will use their minds and bodies as they grow. Common playtime exposes them to behaviors that enable self-reliance. Play is pretended conflict and controlled creation. Its practice runs are necessary to prepare for a world of real consequence. Because reality does not play fair or ease up when its discomfort comes too fast, controlled simulations offer the freedom to explore all possibilities without the threat of long-term repercussions. Play is a type of activity where the outcome of the effort expended does not matter, but the changes to knowledge and personality structure resulting from expending the effort certainly do.

Though we all experience childhood, where we go from there is unpredictable. Aged minds may fail to see the point of new behaviors when they emerge. They cannot recognize the opportunities that exist beyond their inherited limitations. As no one living now can know what human traits the generations to come will require to thrive in the world not yet arrived, learning through play must never be prevented. It is especially important to retain it when the world in which it is retained is increasingly unlikely to retard its rate of changes.

In each new generation, emergent faculties surface atop the foundations of ancient institutions. If we are ever to move outside of their containment, we will need to call on mindsets of playfulness and foolery from time to time as we move about in the world, even (perhaps especially) as serious and aging adults. That way, we will continue to learn, grow, and test what we assumed was true throughout our lives. Our parents could not help but disserve us by failing to push us to rise beyond the patterns they came to live by. They maintained the only paradigms they knew. It was not in their nature to encourage rampant alteration because they did not perceive that anything was wrong with the way they had come to live in the world and that alteration was necessary.

Experience grants us wisdom but often at the cost of gaiety, which is a trait that is seldom given the credit it deserves. Play is a product of our innate curiosity. It makes limitations irresistible and the pushing of them sustainably engaging for our fickle emotions. Adults too fast grow weary of their limits. However, their exploration is not a game but a task imposed upon them, if it happens at all. In that state, change no longer causes excitement in us but stress. Our variety of activity narrows until we, now fully grown, become more of only one thing and less of any other. At last, we are nothing at all but what it is entirely convenient for us to die as.

Some level of childlike innocence throughout the path is key to maintaining a sense of engagement with reality, so protect your sense of wonder like you would protect your life itself. So long as growth excites you, you will always seek new outlets. You will revel in your downtime so you can re-enter the world with emotions reset and abilities upgraded. The alternative is to allow damage and entropy to accumulate, ultimately to surrender to their power over you. Do not underestimate your playful side, as it is the doorway to new personality structures at any stage of development.

To continue expanding well past your juvenile years, take measures now to guard against the loss of playful faculties. Ignore the curmudgeons who retired early from life's games, hardening their hearts, forever releasing their levity. Fun should not be limited to only societally approved categories or activities. A playful mindset is a timeless and principled approach to life. You should adopt it whenever frustration accumulates among your daily stresses, as it is guaranteed to do across time. Find out whatever it is that allows you to become joyfully engaged in what should be stressful barriers you encounter.

When you act merely for the fun of seeing what might happen, each new detail, whatever its source, contributes to your structure. Suffering, while inevitable, does not necessarily make an action more meaningful or your identity any grander once its lessons have been learned. Not all suffering has something valuable to teach you, especially when it is suffering you have already encountered and integrated into your evolving identity. It is okay then to enjoy some aspects of the process.

Your play is your curiosity put into action, and fun is its reward. It is the result of allowing yourself to embody the wonder you have held at the base of your awareness since you were an infant. Practice this beneficial and foolish state whenever the stress of change overtakes you or your fear of the unfamiliar freezes you. Cease it only when you die.

# 14
# Fear and
# Limitation

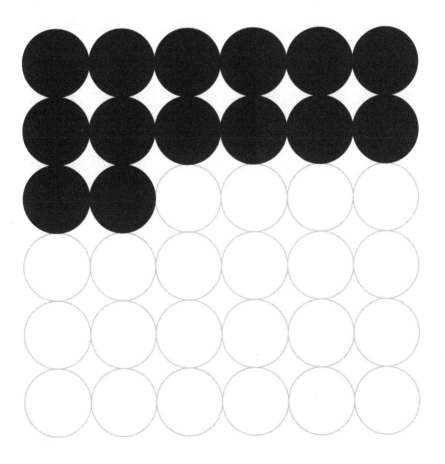

# Fear and Limitation

*The path of meaning is rife with psychological obstacles. Their negating influence upon motivation can make us to hesitate and cower, causing us to doubt our abilities to move beyond what seems risky to the continuation of our comfort and security. Fear is the barrier that determines whether we will move further into or retreat away from the intimidating unknown in every encounter. Fear is what interrupts our ability to act on our developing ideals and the test of our devotion to our principles.*

◆━━━━━━━━━━━━━━◆━━━━━━━━━━━━━━◆

Reality is composed entirely of experiences the mind either has the requisite familiarity to manage or experiences still new enough to overwhelm it. All information a human being is capable of adopting is part of either known or unknown schemas for appropriate interaction. At all times, all people are in a battle to manage the possible chaos of their experience, attempting to turn the tide toward the favor of their comfort. It is their predominantly felt emotions that do the major part of determining how this battle will play out for them.

Fear is an emotional tool, like any other, that has evolved to aid in comfort and survival, to prevent an excess of the unknown and potentially harmful from overwhelming a mind before it is ready to adapt. Fear is the reminder of boundaries not yet crossed. It defends against irreversible error by reminding each person what he cannot do and preventing him from moving where he is not ready to. Fear is natural, preemptive protection from what may cause harm. It is the pressure to stick with what one knows, regardless of curiosity or ambition.

How a person approaches the unmanageable determines the long-term trajectory of his exploration. So long as he feels that he is in control, the unknown instigates a curious and interested response in him. When exploration comes too quickly, however, it creates an overwhelming sense of fear and caution. His emotions signal emergency, even where there might be none. His mind does not know what to do, only that it is not prepared to do it. So, it must either prepare for everything simultaneously or flee so that it requires no preparation at all.

Fear stems from the awareness of the possibility that the unknown may be unfavorable. Curiosity, its opposite, rests in the hope that the unknown might carry positive changes from which its host can grow. These are the forces at work in everyone to determine how to respond to one's own ignorance, and appropriate responses are always necessary because ignorance is unending. Fear, applied appropriately, keeps a person safe from what may harm him, but too much of it is the antagonist to progress.

While we are still growing, we don't yet know reality's inherent limitations or our own. Each generation learns them anew as it rises up in the world, facing distinct challenges in the context of its present era. But we must be ready to analyze on our own terms what is true and valid about whatever novelty we instantly fear. To always back away from what the world has not prepared us to handle is to guarantee that we will always be subject to the same limitations as it, and it will never be congruent with our nature.

In the early stage of life, our caretakers feared more for us than we did for ourselves. They acquired awareness of key non-instinctual dangers through their personal experience. Without the guidance of their influence to limit our exploration, we would almost certainly stumble into problems we had no faculty to manage, and those problems could seriously harm us. Rampant exploration would swiftly be our end. Instead, because of those instilled fears, we suffered only relatively minor injuries and learned important lessons when we tackled more than we were ready for. But now, the burden of maturity is to set our own temperaments and boundaries because we recognize the old external ones are no longer relevant.

More than that, inappropriate fears actively sabotage the primary mechanism of our exceptional expansion and adventure. Fear, when it grows out of our control, spoils our lust for new experience, including those new experiences which would have led to our biggest trials and most critical moral identity lessons. If we are too cautious, we deny all the possible benefits of the infinite unexplored. Our curiosity withers as the unfamiliar looms ever larger in our consciousness. The familiar then crystalizes, permanently narrowing our field of awareness.

We emerge from shelters constructed by familiar parties into vast and unknown territories. Whatever inherited pains we carry, even though we may have never directly experienced them ourselves, still serve to curtail our behavior. How far will we go to replace the effects of adopted experience with ones we generate firsthand? Must we undertake the effort to do this with literally everything the world told us to avoid before we can be sure what the best ways for us to live will be? Essentially, what we must do now is determined by our own metrics the level of injury that is useful for the purposes of living within our limits and abilities.

The first task is to distinguish between the fear that harms and the fear that protects. How does your past experience affect you here in the present? Can you tell what rational fears are there to defend you? You cannot know that your truths are objective or that your meaning is perfect without experimentation, and experimentation requires playing in the unknown. Stay, for a while, with the discomforts that arise when you picture something personally frightening. If you wait long enough, not immediately running from the sirens that go off inside you at the perception of dangers, your fear might quickly cease to matter. If so, you will eliminate the faulty barrier that hypersensitivity placed inside you and gain the ability to venture where before you never could.

Once you understand how any given fear works inside you, you gain the power to master it. You can then prepare for the foreseeable instances where a known fear might overtake and disable you. So, simulate its effects ahead of time. Will yourself into extreme states of panic or despair, imagining as vividly as you can how the worst of all conceivable situations might harm you.

Via prolonged exposure in the mind, can you develop a practical resistance to what harms you? Can you become a more capable actor in the world with a broader range of possible functions?

Old fears need not remain obstacles once you realize their obsolescence (if they ever even played a viable role at all). They can be your doorway to parts of yourself not yet revealed. Whatever is hurting you now may actually evolve to aid you. The deepest pains will eventually be seen as bittersweet because you will know they play vital roles in helping you remember the areas of reality you have been reluctant to explore until now. The stresses you endure are, therefore, a tremendously valuable type of suffering, so long as you can recover from the damage that they inflict to your psyche. In time, the rightful fears will still be there to protect you, while the illusory ones will fade to nothing.

# 15
# Passion and Stimulation

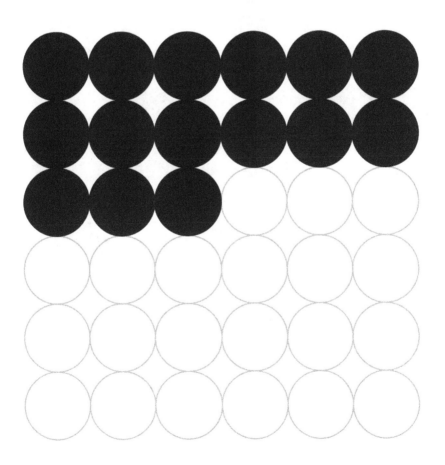

# Passion and Stimulation

*The world, with its overbearing pressure to conform to its passing values, has the persistent tendency to drain fire from the ambition of the exceptional actors forced to move against it. By building our lives around our passions, we can recover a great deal of our lost momentum and, through that, maintain our individuality even under this torrent of pressure to reform away from what is valid and true. Without an adequate source of passion, no matter how well we see the truth about ourselves and the problems of our world, we will eventually run out of motion.*

All emotional impact naturally diminishes across time. Novelty swiftly fades from mind. Out of the many activities that can occupy a waking life, what catches one's attention will differ for each mind according to its unique and natural inclinations. One who looks will quickly discover that there are relatively few pursuits that offer meaningful returns on their investment of time and consciousness required. Passion is the property that retains an interest in familiar things that would otherwise fade from attention. The people who accomplish the greatest deeds in their time are those who stay immersed in their passions for as much of their waking life as possible. Passion is what gives their actions all meaning.

The way of the world is such that, as children, its residents are made to segregate their pursuits by what seems most categorically useful to general mentalities. So, society's adults are products of the values all around them, the invisible influence of which has shaped the very structures by which they learned about themselves and reality herself. They are missing the agency to find their joy or interest without force. They have lost sight of their natural passions, if they ever even had such sight at all.

Only once they learn to master their time might mature adults begin to give up pastimes that do not enable their true identities to emerge further into the world incompatible. Then they might finally begin to see that there are some rare activities that retain influence in them across great passages of time. It is these activities that fuel the heroic flame in them and grant permanence to their earthly identities. Without them, they fade gradually into nothing.

Passion lies in the processes that enable fuller self-expression. Natural passions carry through the injury of obstacles. Curiosity may start the journey, but passion holds its momentum. The most powerful passions nullify interruption in awareness, possessing even the whole body for a time through unignorable stimulation. Passion brings the self-aware person home when he is lost in the worldly maelstrom. Passion breaks the facade projected over him by the collective.

Passion—to care so much about something in a personal way that others cannot necessarily understand—is both impressive and intimidating to the dispassionate, whose lives pass with little meaning or resistance to the greater flow of things. That is why we will be, many times, pressured to forego our potential greatness and why we must learn to focus on what stimulates us when the rest of reality seems to drag us down. Our world will only ever encourage us to excel in a handful of permissible capacities. We will only be allowed to feel special and appreciated for the ways the world prefers for us to stand out within it, merely a few steps beyond the norm and not of a vastly different systemic order than it.

But even having been programmed within the norms and order of the world, we will never quite belong to it. If we continue on their path, though we may subsist and tolerate for a long while, existential dread will, at some time, come to claim us. We will always, on some level, know that the dull gray facsimile the world prefers from us is only a sliver of our potential. Only passion pulls us beyond the world's narrative limitations for us into the greater boundary conditions where we belong. We cannot even know how far out those genuine boundaries are until we reach them.

Authentic passions are rare and specialized for heightened minds, which is why it frequently takes so much exploration to discover them. Our core passions engage us in development, no matter our hardship, defining the priority of our choices and the nuclei of our identities. Knowing this is what gives us clarity for how to act when chaos shrouds the path. The greater our passion, the stronger our endurance against chronic mundane distraction and the more meaning we will retain in our actions regardless of changing emotions.

Society, however, encourages you to make only a limited few areas of interest or activity the focus of your development. It gives you a place in its story. It stops the voice inside you from speaking about what else you could possibly become. But nothing is ever just one thing. Passions can be emergent and complementary, structured to support one another in ways that are not apparent to conventional observers. Whatever has the power to hold your attention while you are alive is central to your growth.

Examine the factors that make activities worthwhile to you. Is it in the way you move your body? The way something tickles your senses? The intellectual faculties you apply as your mind interfaces with reality? The emotions activated? Or the subject matter you explore? Identify your principles of engagement so you can manufacture better methods to apply them. Addiction can be a powerful form of intrigue. In terms of your heroic development, it's never an action in and of itself that matters; it's your mindset about why you're doing it and the meaning you're able to glean. Make it your goal to know the limits of your engagement.

Passion is the only way to unlock all the faculties that define you. Through conscious choice, you expand your abilities to think and feel as the being you really are. Following what engages you will lead to the deepest joys and sorrows that it is within the capacity of your design to know. These are the boundaries of your responses to reality. Alternatively, weak minds seek distraction from the emptiness that lingers in the edges of their perception. They know only mild happiness or mild distress. By venturing into your passionate polarities, you make far more than these weak milestones possible.

But engagement will always carry consequence. The strength of your passion will be tested by how willing you are to endure its inevitable aftermath. If the pain is too great and the rewards too meager, you will question what you thought you cared about. Secure in new knowledge, you will reorient yourself toward a truer version of what sets you free with your passionate expression, and you will be happy to remain there because nothing else could possibly begin to offer the meaningful sensations that a life away from mediocrity has shown you.

# 16
# Intellect and Isolation

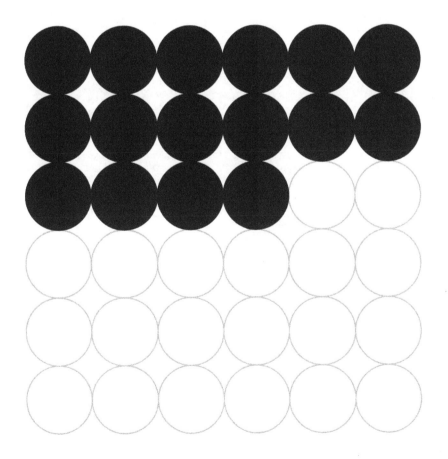

# Intellect and Isolation

*All minds that pursue refinement of the lenses through which they interpret existence face isolation from those that never complete a similar cerebral journey. Our understanding of reality and self depends upon the sharpening of our minds through upgraded categories, senses, and the philosophies we generate. We cannot expect the world to appreciate what new meaning we discern or what we become as our interpretations drift far too far from what it can consider. For thinking creatures such as us, a degree of alienation is certain.*

The way a person thinks about the universe is always a simulation of an actually unknowable reality. His perception cannot ever be truly passive. He always adds a bit of himself to what he sees and interacts with in each moment. He makes guesses informed by prior experience about what is going on in front of him and projects them wildly onto his world. His talent is constructing conceptual outlines, which, though extraordinarily useful to him, he often mistakes for genuine articles. Such is the role of the intellect: to give the mind the means to navigate the world via useful representation of it.

Intellect is intimately connected to the emotions, not counter to or detached from them. Indeed, all meaning springs from their combined overlay upon experience. From meaning, all goals become possible. Win states become definable. Destiny becomes inevitable, for it is the product of how one thinks, feels, and acts upon reality.

As processing evolves, even though the world itself may remain the same, the mind ceases to recognize the world that it began in and what it used to be. It loses identification with other minds that cannot rise to meet it, which shuns it from its former herd. Each new step it takes is a step away from averageness and normality, away from any way to continue belonging to the collective by its default qualities.

Skill, wealth, and influence are nothing without an intelligent mind to manage them. Intellect is what leverages them for gain. Intellect accumulates, builds upon itself when other things degrade. Intelligence is a source of emergent growth because it dips into the unknown and slowly makes it known. Its nature is to integrate the old and new, refining structures out of chaos.

Ultimately, any human trait may be celebrated or condemned by the society it is part of, and society's response strongly influences how we express our traits. Through chronic reinforcement, the world relegates us to only what is useful about us to the norm. Therefore, we, the outliers who do not fit well into society's forms, grow ashamed of how we perceive ourselves apart from it. The original insights we work so hard to formulate cannot be spread to minds not qualified to receive them, so the more we create, the further isolated we will feel.

If we are good learners with high capacities for adaptive reason, we will find that many forms of specialization are within our cognitive capabilities to pursue. We can adapt ourselves to a wide berth of unrelated areas that hold our interest because we have enhanced perception to see them clearly. We, therefore, face a greater burden of choice for how to relate to human civilization and fill our roles within it.

Ironically, intelligence is the only trait that must be held in great capacity to be understood to a great degree. This truth is inescapable because intellect is the means through which all conceptualization occurs and which all traits are analyzed. After all, intelligence is the faculty to make consistent meaning from experience and the mechanism for categorizing all adopted data.

The power to think at levels far beyond ordinary perception tends to challenge mainstream assumptions about the nature and function of humanity. The paths we pick might alienate us from the institutions we depend on to survive. To the unintellectual, rapid learning feels to be a form of dark wizardry. The quick mind arrives at outcomes without any visible means of navigation behind the destination. It seems a sleight of hand or cheating, something fundamentally unfair because it is not available to every player in the game. So, the most advanced thinkers are discouraged from bringing the operations of their minds out into the world where they would create much-needed order.

Chronically denied the opportunity to share our intellects, we begin to feel alien among our kind. We even begin to lose our desire to learn, for we identify it as the source of our worsening anguish and isolation. Feeling disempowered, we either cut ourselves off from our great capacity for seeing the hidden operations of ordinary things or become obsessed with using it to acquire greater power for short-sighted and destructive ends.

Your emergent future depends upon your intellectual abilities, as your intuition and emotional knowledge run only on the past they have so far encountered. They cannot be spontaneously calibrated to new circumstances that result from a complex state of emergent evolution when countless seemingly familiar factors interact to produce something foreign. Intuition merely forms unconscious associations from the experience it knows. But reason can do what intuition does not: rapidly deconstruct the emergent unfamiliar for assimilation. Reason integrates the absurd until it is absurd no longer.

Divergent minds like yours find ways to bring resolution to disorder because they see solutions for order that other minds cannot. Your superior awareness drives you to innovate beyond the limits of your peers. But you can only do this if you accept the truth of your advanced cognition. Focus on your intellectual progress long enough, and you'll go places none before you have even known it was possible to go. You'll become as resourceful, persistent, and unwavering as your intellect allows you to. You will change the disorderly things out there in reality to how your mind knows they ought to be for the sake of order and virtue.

You will, however, still grow to feel isolated from minds with normal filters. The way you perceive things will be too different from any norm. Your mind works in ways unique to you. How information accumulates in you forms your paradigm, your unique way of interpreting the world. Your fated social disparity will lead to either quiet desperation or rapid innovation.

The world only ever celebrates the genius it has the space to accommodate. People will always resist you if your insight threatens the accepted order of their lives, and you displace them from their castes. And so long as you continue to sacrifice your intellectual growth for social convenience, you will never know what you can become. So, be strong enough to maintain your intellect as a priority in the face of cultural pushback. One day, with persistence and countless new generations affected by those like you who heroically persevered, the strange but superior become the new norm, raising the tide for everyone.

# 17
# Creativity
# and Reform

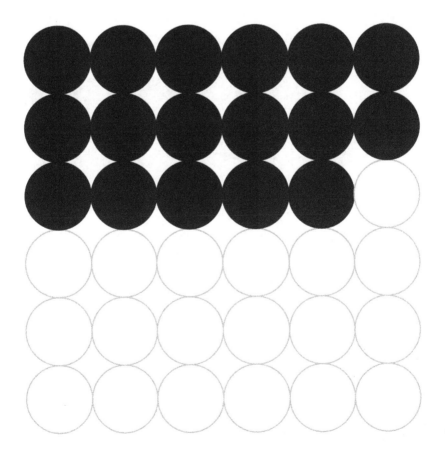

# Creativity and Reform

*A sharp mind is not sufficient to succeed on the path out of banality into meaning. For problems that have no readily deducible solutions under our acclimated states of knowledge, novel forms of creative thinking may be required. To tackle such problems, we must hold onto our capacity to apply old strategies in new ways and question all unspoken assumptions about how the most basic aspects of the universe we think we know might actually operate. Fully unleashing our creativity is the key to willfully rearranging the filters through which we experience and then analyze ourselves and our reality.*

---

The value of a mind does not alone reside in its capacity to organize what it perceives. More than a filing system, a mind builds new meaning from reality's raw materials. What a mind knows is never the end to what it is able to know, even when working from the same basic variables. This is because the world humans navigate is not composed of elements aloft in isolation. Reality's emergent possibilities, birthed anew in every moment, cannot all be explored within a single given lifetime by even the most endowed individual. No person can know all there is to know about even a single subject. Furthermore, he cannot even know a single fact that is not dependent upon another prior fact. His intellect is always limited, so he depends upon creative growth to avoid stagnation.

Creative growth is easiest while young. A child's imagination is inspiring to adults because it lacks the discipline to separate the inherent from the invented. Unlike the embittered adult who is ashamed to let his creative mind wander, the child is eager to develop his own uncommon meaning. He, heroically, never stops himself from applying his will to reality. It is an automatic process for him, one that will be gradually ironed flat by a world that tolerates less and less of his spontaneous creation as he ages.

Creative thinking can make a mind immune to the chaos of a crisis. The thoughts of a creative mind adapt to no end. The artist does not right away lose his identity when familiar meaning fails to support his pursuits and bring him the answers his quests require. He reforms any intellectual debris creatively to suit his present needs. He builds new worlds as needed just as quickly as the old ones wither.

All creation requires the creator to perceive past normal places of resistance. Innovators must capitalize gainfully on the novel patterns they discover. Intellect may be what delineates reality, placing what it knows into containers to be tapped as situations call for them, but creativity pushes them to break or merge, even when doing so yields no immediate reward. Intelligence without the perspective of its limits becomes a closed loop of circular thinking. But to think creatively is to push a mind beyond its limits into the emerging unknown.

Yet, no matter how formidable our creative strengths might feel, we will always be subject to various forms of creative decay. Our old knowledge quickly becomes our creative enemy when it contradicts our freshest experience, so we must frequently make compromises between the two. The ideas we find useful at one point on the path begin to solidify and prevent us from discovering what else we might become or how else we might be able to see the world. Even if we can mostly avoid the world's constraining influence, we might just as easily become prisoners in cages we construct for ourselves from our habits and routines. Once it becomes familiar to think and do things a certain way, any novel arrangement must compete.

Unavoidably, creation grows more difficult for us as we dull from repetition. We cease our once-rapid expansion and begin to implement strange emotional restraints upon ourselves and even upon each other. If we cannot apply our minds creatively with ongoing consistency, we succumb to unconscious acts of self-destruction for the stimulation they provide. We fester our ambition, which, once corrupted, might never allow us to reclaim our lost potential.

The conventional mind, pursuing comfort, surrounds itself with appeals to its familiar preferences. Under its influence, we fear what we could become, which limits our actually vast focus to a spotlight of our creative possibilities. If we do not allow ourselves to practice our creativity, it will become limited to what other minds afford us. We will remain unable to formulate our knowledge into arrangements any more profoundly than those who gave us the knowledge to begin with. This hardening of our creativity blinds us to undiscovered parts of reality, the arrangements of which we know are not the entire story. But when we enable our comfort to expand beyond this to new arrangements, our creativity expands along with it.

Under stagnant mental layouts, your thinking halts early at arbitrary places. A single misaligned category can ruin the accuracy of your perception. Even an altered premise can deconstruct all previously known outcomes. A creative epiphany such as this is the sudden realigning of familiar ideas into novel categories. It reveals emergent properties for you to wander. It turns even the most familiar territory into something undiscovered.

Still, as your mind cannot interpret anything without the helping bias of your memories, the remembered past will always have a constraining hold on you. Only via acts of new creation can you build anew the means by which you interpret even your memories and, thus, your present thoughts and actions too. Hold in your mind the premise that no matter the obstacle, a thousand unconsidered possibilities exist outside the scope of your habitual perception.

Your mind loves to assign purpose to its information, but none of your knowledge is limited to the purposes you assign it. Creativity frees you from this trap by filing your conceptions down to their constituent elements and rearranging them, showing you that the way you chose to see something before was never the only way you could have seen it. Whenever reality seems to lack new stimulation to keep you invested in its outcome, you may still conjure your own novelty through creative rearranging of what you know.

Train yourself to look upon the familiar parts of reality with eyes never told how to see them. Through recognizing the useful principles at the base of reality's structures, you will find greater opportunity to alchemize one thing into another. You will gain access to outcomes unending when you arrange familiar things in new patterns and unleash their emergent properties into the universe. There are, after all, more sides to reality than you will ever know.

# 18
# Consistency and Understanding

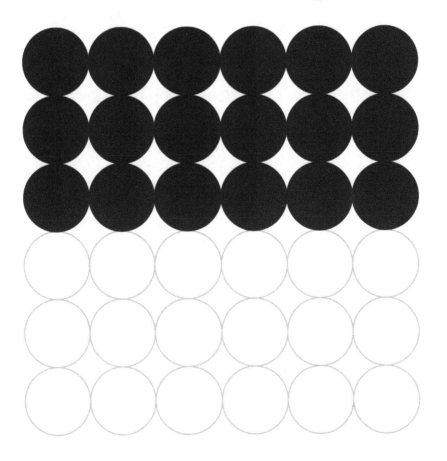

# Consistency and Understanding

*The pursuit of an orderly mind is to make structure out of what chaos persists all around it. In the course of this pursuit, we each do our part to pull the world a little more toward its ideal state and bring enlightenment to the dark. We make the collecting of knowledge our ally, submitting ourselves to new ideas constantly and adding to our paradigms. We evaluate each new piece of evidence or proposition to arrive at better understanding because we know the truth is where our allegiance should always take us. Anything less is a betrayal of our character.*

A mind's power derives wholly from its owner's ability to wield it. The adaptive mind applied well brings reality together in sometimes shockingly unobvious ways. It applies a consistent system of order across all things unconnected, revealing the connections that were present all along. It knows that truth is the universal unifier that must be shared by all things equally without aberration. Only the incredibly vain believe that it is within their human mandate to apply exclusive rules to portions of reality they cannot integrate with the whole. When their invented rules do not reflect what they encounter, they insist it is reality that must be wrong. They seek supremacy over all.

Forever at work, human minds sort stimuli into categories that they have been formulating since their earliest base experiences. But, to be consistent and true, they must never take it upon themselves to force ideas into containers to which they do not belong. When one's categories are inadequate to account for all their information about reality, psychological conflict is inevitable. The mind must then choose to reduce or expand itself in response to the apparent contradiction.

So long as expansion prevails in the face of warring ideas, the worldview of the individual can never really lose. It will eventually arrive at a better framework to think and live by. But should arrogance prevail and the strain of thinking appear too great, the mind will opt to reduce itself instead to a simpler state where thoughts that oppose cannot stretch it any longer. Gradual self-destruction becomes its destiny.

It is the uniquely apt human capacity for reason that turns curiosity viable and idle thinking actionable. The ability to think clearly is the only defense that exists against ignorant thought and action that pervades the world with its endless destructive consequences for humanity. Only if one should embrace the ability to acquire deep and consistent understanding will the broken rules that order typical mindless thinkers to an early intellectual demise no longer matter. Only the principled and dedicated thinker can remake the forms that hold the world afloat in thinking human minds before they move the products of human civilization to crumble.

Each of us must remain free to make sense of what we perceive in the world around us as we grow ever more into it. If we cannot organize new revelations as we acquire them, exploration dies in us early, long before we ever have the opportunity to see the heights to which it would have taken us.

Strange things remain intimidating because they have no means by which to join our internal architecture. No integration ever occurs between the old and new, so foreign things stay foreign, and we stay as prisoners of our old ways of seeing the world.

Though few of us are self-analytical enough to acknowledge them, we all rely on our own rules to navigate the invisible spaces of our minds and the visible spaces of our world daily. Without principles to our thinking, our minds branch, without discretion or form, in every direction, and even basic accumulation never occurs. There is no hierarchy, no absolute metric of validity to contrast our thoughts with. So long as we live this way, we are only spectators in our own minds. We play no active role in shaping the flow of understanding.

When truth lies beyond our mental boundaries, we cease to think about it freely. Life becomes a downward spiral, and we are forced to fit ourselves within a space not made for growth or exploration. Our categories become our prisons. So, when we see that we can progress no further in new knowledge under our old assumed premises, we must take it upon ourselves to step away from our dead ends and faulty strategies. There is no use in repeating our mistakes simply because we are too stubborn to perceive them for what they are. We should, instead, reinterpret the premises of our foundational understanding and take less for granted about what we assume. Then, we may realize that there is no knowledge not to be questioned and no assumptions not to be shaken. Reality will never change to accommodate our limits.

In every situation, there is more than one way to interpret your experience. You, like everyone else, rely on your mind to bridge the known and the inferred. Whenever an idea enters your mentality, your burden is to determine its validity but not randomly, arbitrarily, or inconsistently. This is an ongoing battle that only grows more difficult as it becomes clear that other minds will never stop trying to make you think as they do, regardless of your differing experience. The truth must align with your observation of it and be immune to mental strong-arming.

When you arrive at the truth by your own principled methods, do not expect any others to understand why your path has brought you to that destination. You perform disservice to yourself by awaiting their agreement or approval. After all, your experiences are uniquely your own. A masterful thinker and communicator may be gifted enough to share a significant portion of what he knows. Still, even he should never expect another person to be able to hold the same awareness that he has earned through methodical mental tinkering. You alone are responsible for what comes to thrive in your understanding because you are always the one undergoing the effort to arrive there.

Your extended capacity to think clearly not only enables you to see the universe into forms more useful and consistent but also to act in ways to make it more congruent with your values. Once you can apply your mind with this purpose as your motivation, reason moves you closer to the world you wish to be a part of, but it only works when you do not rely on external authorities to tell you how reality works or ought to work. With an honest desire for understanding, whatever the cost, at your side, you can expand your knowledge in any manner that captures your interest and begin to take the actions of the person you foresee yourself to be.

Understanding arrives through patience and principle. Hone your ability to see the relationships between all things. Identify their workings. Retain the perception that there is always space to improve and a chance to be wrong. Master yourself first by seeking purity and universal truths as the basis for your paradigm, and eventually master your heroic influence upon your world.

# 19
# Sensitivity and Perception

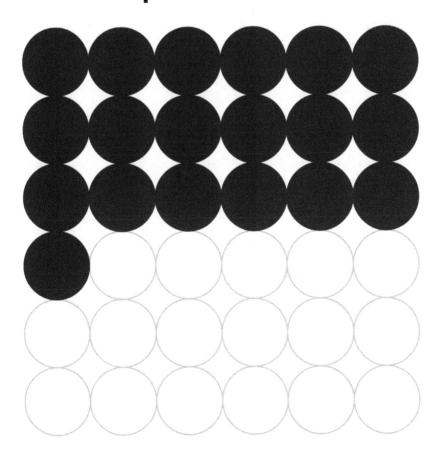

# Sensitivity and Perception

*The world exists in a perpetual state of needing saving. The burden to save it falls on those of us who are attuned to the need, we who can see what others cannot. But how and to what extent we will notice its stabbing layers of brokenness vary with each individual. There are finite tolerable limits to each of us and our perception. We can never act upon everything we process nor process everything there is. A hierarchy of if and how to act on our awareness quickly forms. What we find meaningful is clearly shaped by what we are most sensitive to.*

◆———————————————◆

What a person believes is necessary for him to do with his perceivable universe is influenced by the amount of universe he is capable of perceiving. The most sensitive thinkers notice even the unexamined motivators that rest beneath the conscious choices ordinary people think of as their own. They continue to pay attention to every fraction of physical motion happening all around them, even when others quickly filter it out. To see the hidden influence in all things is enough to drive even a capable mind mad if it is not ready for such an informational load. To witness the world's motions, to hear its hustle and its noises in every waking moment, grants a mind an entirely different experience of even the same basic stimuli.

Ironically, increased communication and social awareness often leads to the perceiver having to conceal his perception so as not to come across as strange or invasive, which only adds to the chronic trouble of fitting in and functioning. Even through something as innocuous as the heightened awareness of speech patterns and body language, unconscious desires may be noticed when they are otherwise totally hidden, thus granting an automatic level of intimacy for all human encounters. Estrangement is the price for not perceiving human behavior on the shallow level intended or the meaning of reality the same as the masses. Yet, it is the same trait that might lead to being celebrated, so long as the mind can find a way to transmute its base ingredients into products of worldly commendation.

Over time, the sensitive receiver may almost entirely lose the ability to take for granted the once-hidden causes that are now, in all things, obvious. He cannot ignore or forget what he sees and recalls every time he looks out there into the overwhelming and non-working world. There are curtains he can never fully close. He sees the gears and workings, even when doing so does not seem to aid him. This sensitivity is the primary stage of his signature creativity, intellect, and insight, as it gathers the building blocks upon which his mind applies its impressive efforts.

Though we might, sometimes, feel gratitude for taking in more profound beauty in so-called ordinary things than ordinary people ever can, perception works in both directions. When things all around us seem fine to normal eyes, ours might see that there are endless strategic errors, broken systems, or suffering souls calling for emergency attention. Worse still, the world around us may treat us as though there is something egregious and contemptible about pointing out to them the seriousness of what is going on and with wondering out loud why no one feels inclined to act on it as we do.

Over time, everyday encounters require ever stronger effort from us if we are to observe and mimic the acceptable range of actions demonstrated by our peers. We know from experience that the moment we fail to respond appropriately to positive or negative feedback from those we interact with and especially social authority figures, our survivability in this capricious social environment falls drastically. We cannot truly get along in a world that we do not receive the same as the rest of its populace.

Enhanced senses allow perpetual irritants into the cellars of our consciousness. With sharper eyes and minds set to notice all the world's broken ways, it becomes impossible to ignore the disorder we all live in, even when others seem to do so without effort. Should any of our senses become so sharp that we cannot ignore the stream of information they bring to us, they may damage our overall ability to conceive of the world usefully. Consequently, our perceptual gifts will prevent us from acting in ways accordant with our values. The information that should be helping us optimize our behavior instead becomes a major obstacle. What good is heightened perception when the noise of reality only serves to conquer us and beat us to submission?

Hypersensitivity leads to a loss of confidence in our discernment about what is real, what is serious, and what requires our intervention. And once we cease to believe in the validity of our natural senses, we nullify our ability to ride the line that separates order from destruction and bring our values out from within us. Since there is only so much we can do to dull perception, we are likely to live out our lives in suffering about the situations that require us to act but that we feel powerless to actually influence. Awareness lacking action is hell or limbo, and it is profoundly unheroic.

Being sensitive to your environment need not forever be a curse for you. More than anything, it is a responsibility, a calling to interact with the world on a higher level on account of how you experience it. Part of the very reason you are drawn to take on grand heroic efforts ignored by others is, indeed, because you cannot help but notice how those efforts have so far gone unfulfilled in the world. It is your perspective that has shaped your way of being in the world and defined the quests that are you are starting to see as yours alone to follow. That which you uniquely pay attention to is what colors your unique experience.

You will probably never have the luxury of closing your eyes or shutting your brain off to the world's erratic motions. When others think that all is fine and there is nothing urgently wrong, you will perceive the countless signals that insist that it is otherwise. You will hear the voices calling out for aid, even if they are inaudible to everyone who does not share your burden. You will zero in on unnecessary suffering so that you can begin to eliminate what could so easily be avoided if people were just capable of singling out its cause the way you do. Your sensitivity to strife makes you better suited to remedy the burdens people carry, thereby helping them to live more orderly. You enable them, in turn, to focus on what good they too could create in the world, no longer haunted by the ghosts of traumas past and evils sprouted by emotions unresolved.

What once you perceived to be a burden can be the impetus for you to evolve to higher levels of heroism, elevating you ever closer to where you would be had you been born into a world adequate for sensitive souls and minds receptive of great detail. Because you are designed to still perceive when others have lapsed in their attention, the responsibility is now naturally yours to make up for their worldly failings, even if they can never notice or appreciate you because your efforts exist beneath the scope of their ill-functioning radar. There is no escaping your nature. All you must learn to do is embrace it in some manner that gives you purpose and enables you to function in a world that assaults your senses.

# 20
# Responsibility and Judgment

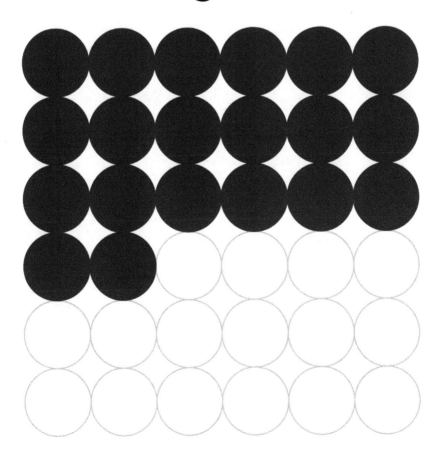

# Responsibility and Judgment

*Humanity's judgment applied upon reality, if it is just and reasonable, appeals to something greater than its wielder's bias or desire. Operating in such a judicial manner, we question how we came upon the conclusions we have made about how reality is and ought to go. We navigate backward in our minds to reconsider the origins of our evaluations in order that we may judge singularly by standards that do not change with circumstance or wavering emotion. Then, we will take responsibility for and stand beside every choice we ever make, even when things don't turn out the way we aim them to.*

No person can live without interpreting his environment, and every interpretation is an application of his personal judgment. Ordinarily, judgment is applied so quickly that it completely lacks any conscious discretion. People fall into habits of investing their biases heavily into everyday events of no real consequence to their goals. These judgments silently affect them, manipulating their reactions to all that exists around them. It is, ultimately, an enormous drain on their emotional and cognitive resources, and it keeps them from seeing things fairly. But in each moment, minds of ample self-awareness also have the choice to continue to live as slaves to their automated evaluations or take control of their own judgment.

A person who takes responsibility for what he overlays onto reality develops greater confidence in his standards for how he believes reality should be, as he manages to retain the awareness that those standards belong to him alone and not the objects he is assessing. He trusts the validity of his reading because he learns, through ongoing trial and error, what it means to be righteous, to be good, to be fair, and to be just. He has done so much more than accept these vague but pleasant ideas as unexamined premises to all behavior and his very own identity.

Judgment, however wise, can never reach perfection. A good judge knows it is always necessary to base his reactions on imperfect information, as knowledge itself can never be perfect. To pretend otherwise is hubris. Those who do not trust their own judgment wait until a clear and obvious path appears because they do not want to be the ones tasked with the responsibility of deciding which, out of infinite possible directions, is the correct one to take, either morally or logistically. They especially cannot bear the consequences of judging wrongly when much is the line and when their errors in judgment mean significant losses for themselves and others.

Only if one is courageous enough to practice his ability to interpret the worth of human actions will he act with a confidence that is earned even when others only pretend to or fail to act at all. Only he will see in a way that carries weight when a course of action is warranted, even when others are blind to it. He will correct imbalances as soon as they occur in his observation. He will be the savior the present crisis demands him to be without sacrificing who he is or forcing him to doubt his heroic values.

When we only know one way of seeing things, we forget that not everyone shares our values or perspectives. We may see ourselves as artists and our world as an endless series of outlets for our creative expression. We may like-wise think ourselves to be intellectuals, contemplating the world as ordered systems that have empowered us to manipulate it to our will. But still, we take for granted the fact that the way we see things is not a perfect represen-tation of the way they are. We are always applying our own biases, which will never be entirely identical to the biases of someone else. So, our experience of reality will never be quite like theirs.

When we attribute meaning to what exists in our awareness, we open our-selves to the harsh internal consequences of the standards we set for it. Our judgments quickly accumulate, to the point we can no longer even identi-fy where they began. Soon, other minds respond to our palpable critiques. They stack their own atop the pile of meaning that we have generated and carry around with us as we continue observing the universe. This cumulative superstructure of collective meaning is responsible for the maelstrom of hu-man emotion we experience in society every day. It is the catalyst for count-less chaotic human reactions to all things imaginary and invented. After a time, only the most steadfast minds retain the ability to tell the difference between what is real and what has been imbued upon the real.

Conventional minds apply pressure to corral our judgment when it matters most so that we never risk stepping outside the collective approach to evalua-tion or offending anyone. They believe that we, as lone individuals, can never be strong enough to carry the responsibility of discretion in our hearts. They fear that even their own power will inevitably lead them to destruction, and so, they never practice their judiciary facilities in any individual capacity that matters. They hope we never grow adept or gain mastery over the meaning we place upon reality. They would prefer that we continue to outsource truth to social authorities that come in a thousand different forms.

To embrace responsibility for your judgment is to make amends for when it turns out to be wrong. It is to spend the remainder of your life on a quest to find and mend your flawed assumptions that have led to flawed action or in-action. You especially have an obligation to make recourse when your errors impair another person. Willing restitution is the price you pay to maintain your virtue as a heroic soul interacting with the world on exclusively righ-teous terms. It is your task to extend your empathy to the appropriate degree and see your interactions from the perspective of all you interact with.

Taking responsibility for your judgment is not just the morally right thing to do; it is even essential to attaining the higher levels of your continued existential development. Failure to take dominion over everyday decisions prevents you from applying your judgment to things larger and more worth-while. To seek large goals, you must first upgrade your capacity for determin-ing right action from wrong action incrementally. Heroism is realizing that there is nothing you do that does not matter, whether there are witnesses or visibly significant effects from them or not.

Make it your task to take on new, somewhat less insignificant tasks each day of your life. See them to completion. Dedicate yourself to an outcome where you can safely judge some state of things to be better by the metric of your principles due to the direct involvement of your behavior. Do this so long as you are willing to bear the consequences when, despite your best efforts, you make mistakes, and your judgment turns out wrong. Apply your critical review wherever you can manufacture a meaningful impact upon a situation and witness the result. This way, you will feel the full impact of emotional rewards and punishments appropriately.

Your discretion is heroic when it provides protection from chaos. It is your primary weapon against disorder and the means by which you know the best possible way for you to interact with the world. Do not fear any longer the segregation of reality into good behavior and bad within the context of your actions. Exert your preference for how things ought to be, but never be satisfied that your preference is perfect or final. Someday soon, you will be ready to be the caretaker of a microcosm of your own systemic order in the making.

# 21
## Will and
## Action

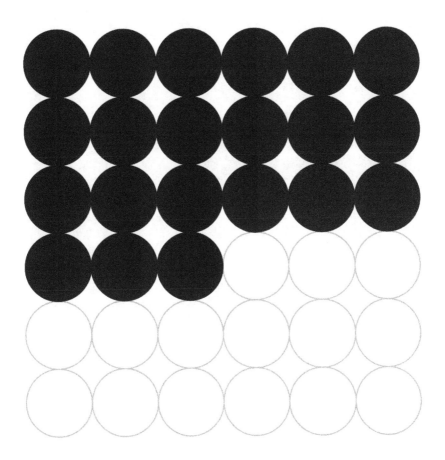

# Will and Action

*Out from the comfort of mind, it is necessary to venture into and apply meaningful ideas throughout reality's shared spaces. We apply our will to tasks we find engaging to make our actions meaningful. We come to see that we should implement our principles into every aspect of our behavior and cognition, or else our developing ideals will never settle, neither within nor outside of us in the world we inhabit. Our willpower wisely acted on, our hands become the instruments of effecting our ambitions and cementing our progress.*

◆———————————————◆

Every asset has its cost, and every contextual advantage can become a disadvantage when context swiftly changes. Without the power to apply oneself meaningfully in the manner suited to one's strengths, those strengths become tremendous burdens. To be able to conceive of goals that would bring deep and specific peace to one's life but lack the proclivity to pursue them is a shallow kind of hell for exceptional individuals. Perpetual unfulfillment, the kind that rots a mind from within, corrupts the very traits that set the exceptional apart from their social norms.

From anyone who expects much from reality, much too is required in return to resolve the weight of his expectations. The longer he stays passive, the more difficult it grows to break free from idleness and begin again to follow his ambitions. His greatness is only achieved by his active intervention in the trajectory of his world, not his passive analysis about or disagreement with it. Few gifted people are naturally prepared to bear the responsibility of their brilliance in all its forms, but all their faculties mean nothing without the will to act on them. Eventually, the lack of will to act upon ambition leads to the lack of will to even live at all.

Habitual dreamers never live to see their ideas tested on rough surfaces. They live out their lives in psychological prisons, never honoring their ambition with will and action. When ambition stretches further than the familiar, the failure to pursue it taints its host's resolve. He will not develop the confidence to attempt the challenges that excite him. The greater the distance between where his mind is and where it can dream of ever heading, the deeper will be the misery that arises from his awareness of the difference. All existential longing develops from this unrealized ambition.

Wandering aloft, lacking a target to align to, we tend to only take on the tasks that require the smallest amount of our limited available effort to conquer. We risk almost nothing on trivial activities. But our high-functioning minds cannot long sustain without a purpose to their processes. Those strong emotions that granted us our initial levels of engagement with reality cannot stay only as emotions forever. They must be converted into equally strong actions before we lose the motivating influence they have upon our willpower.

We easily forget that a struggle over scarcity defines our entire physical universe. No one can be in two places at once, nor can two objects share the same space simultaneously. When we voice and act upon our principles, we

119

necessarily aggress against ideals incompatible. We fight to claim the spaces they occupy. No matter what we proclaim, we do so in opposition to opposite proclamations. In these moments of conflict or disagreement, our will may begin to falter.

Skilled philosophers often hesitate because action invites resistance that does not exist in the intangible realm of philosophy. Ideas do not return any friction to their origin. But when we activate our bodies, we push against the fabric of reality herself. Nothing yields without cost. By willfully existing, we create new order within the entropic flow of all things grander and more powerful than we could imagine. We become part of the great cosmic dispute for dominion during the time we are alive.

Inevitably, we will make mistakes when we try to accomplish what our ambition commands of us, sometimes mistakes so severe that recovery seems impossible. We will feel the pain of injury and error for a while. We will want to quit when the resistance of staying true to our principles seems to grow too strong to endure. We will struggle and fail more times than we can count, or else we will not be even living. Those moments will test our character. Regardless, from the aftermath, we will build ourselves up to be better than before. With every failure, we will set ourselves on course for stronger victories over what is incompatible with our purpose.

In your most agonizing psychological moments, you may have wished for a quick end to your suffering by willful lobotomy so that you would finally be capable of being content with the state of mediocrity like seemingly everyone around you. You may have craved to just be normal, to be removed from responsibility and allowed to experience the world like everyone else. But know that yours is not a hopeless case. With training, you will feel disempowered by your exceptional mind no longer.

An aspirational hero who never steps into reality's arena never completes his journey. He remains forever unborn and undeveloped. So, move consciously toward whatever in the world requires your intervention, for it is the doorway to growth beyond your daydreams. With daily reinforcement, your will becomes as iron, warping the space all around you according to its function. When you voice a strong opinion or act in some exceptional manner, you make yourself psychologically naked. When you demonstrate your values in the public eye, the world will judge the meaning of your actions. There will always be someone to oppose you. It takes character to stand your ground when society moves against you.

If the whole of the world should ever raise its arms against you, endure for the sake of what you know is true in spite of them. Allow yourself the rewards of accomplishment when your will prevails against obstacle. This will add meaning to your time. Meaning is the satiation of the emptiness of existence, which only comes to you by enacting your ambitions. Ignore meaning and resign yourself to a life of idle suffering. If you know your principles inside and out, your body conforms to enact them upon the world. Mold your life as much as you can to match the ideals you have always wished existed on a greater scale in the systems all around you.

With enough practice of aligning your actions to your will, you become confident enough to stand proud as what you are, complete with your own heroic yet idiosyncratic values to define you. You may find in these moments that you are still standing alone. But you should lament not if this turns out to be the case. Even one real example of greatness can activate latent exceptional potential in other souls who witness your existence. It can inspire them to move a little closer to the golden ideal within them that they have so far been too weak to bring out of the shadows of their psyches. Persist with your willful action, and you may yet not have to stand alone forever.

# 22
# Priority and Discretion

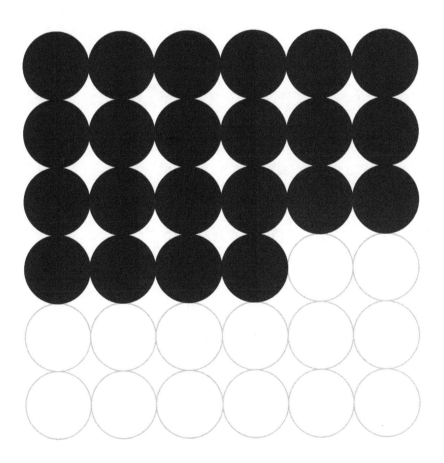

# Priority and Discretion

*One who is on a mission cannot help but see that sometimes problems are beyond his capabilities to solve at once, together, or even in the order he encounters them. Daily, we navigate a world that is the consequence of the shortcomings of our predecessors who left behind the issues they were unable or unwilling to resolve in their time. Since we cannot upend the broken world we were born to, we can only optimize our behavior within its dysfunctioning systems. If we do not craft a tolerable place for ourselves, we will soon or later lose our sanity and resolve.*

━━━━━━━━━━━━━━━━━━━━━

No matter the circumstances of a life, the holder of it cannot help but constantly move to alter them. He remains forever in motion, never at total rest in his body or his mind. To rest completely would be to allow himself to die. So, he is always seeking another point of resistance to surpass. Past that point is where all meaningful progress for his development occurs. But, as he cannot change everything he might ever wish to change and overcome every possible difficulty, he must learn to be selective about the battles he will wage.

Resistance presents a major paradox because it creates a feeling that is somewhere between attraction and repulsion. People naturally fall into patterns dedicated to the avoidance of uncomfortable pressures. They resist each new barrier they encounter, preferring to fill their hours with tasks they already know and mastered long ago. But when they finally know their values, weaknesses, and abilities, they can structure their lives around the breaking of the selective places of resistance that intrigue them.

As problems are an inherent part of how minds perceive reality, people can either languish in the process of having to figure out the order and importance of their resolution or take joy in it. They typically don't realize that they are forging a better internal hierarchy whenever they must choose which issues weigh most heavily on them and must take precedence over others. Any newly solved problem is inevitably followed by problems anew, but a purposeful mind finds meaning in the ongoing cycle. It scales up to better obstacles and, therefore, reaps greater rewards by resolving them. It knows its identity and its place in the world because it knows how it must act in it.

Resistance that recurs in a life unlocks hidden principles and values that might under easier times never have been known, as victory only comes when the most subjectively significant problems clear away from view. The issues that occupy the largest portion of a person's limited attention represent what he most cares about. Their resolution is his peace, his path to a personal nirvana.

There exists a narrow band of comfortable experience that defines the ways that we can function in the world. If we step outside that range a little, the outcome is discomfort. If we step too far, the outcome is destruction. So, we fall into patterns of daily solving problems we've addressed countless times in days before. We navigate mostly fixed tracks, confronting identical frustrations time and again, only ever attaining temporary resolution before the next iteration meets us. We build our lifestyles around the minor challenges that we know we can handle, banal mundanities of no serious consequence.

The stress of solving trivial matters becomes our favorite form of entertainment. Stress gives the idle mind something to occupy it, which is preferable to ever letting itself run empty. But if we should choose to solve our problems systemically instead of incidentally, we would free our minds to fill the emptiness with stresses of greater meaning because they represent greater subjective importance. We would begin to think about what problems we would prefer to solve if only we were more confident and capable of doing so.

It is primarily the timescale through which we analyze our lives that determines how quickly we grow into versions of ourselves capable of living in greater accordance with our ideals. Our intelligent minds can project, to some extent, into the predictable future. They know their problems will recur until they alter the conditions that created them. This is when we begin to take ownership of the principles of our lives, beyond our momentary stimuli. We nullify problems at their origins when we make the conscious choice that there are other matters in the universe that should hold a higher priority for the identities we project ourselves to embody.

Observe the issues that make up the predictable patterns in your life. Ask why today you still have many of the same complaints you have had for as long as you can remember. Is it really these lifestyle mundanities that define you more than the ambitions set by your exceptional design? You can already see what a depressing prognosis that would be were it to turn out to be the case that such soul-sucking errands would stick with you for all your time here. No, there must be something more to your pursuits than this.

The key is to focus on the underperforming principles of your life, not the symptoms that they generate. When you address your issues holistically, you'll free up time you once wasted just managing the effects of your systemic inefficiency. You will tend to a superior crop of problems that appeal far more heavily to the design of your core concerns about the state of your reality. So, while they may at first seem like greater burdens, their rewards too will be appropriately greater. You'll have graduated to a higher level of operation for heroically improving the world, bit by bit.

There is no end to this path of escalating priorities, no permanent plateau to rest on except to learn to be content with solving life's new problems as they arise and to find a place to fit them into your hierarchy as you identify the principal level of importance represented by each ordeal. No matter how good you get at structuring your life around what appeals best to your filter, there will always be personal peaks and valleys, struggles and victories, and these are what make progress worthwhile.

Choose now the nature of the problems that will concern you, and resist the pull to give irrelevant obstacles the bulk of your attention. Problems contaminate the population of humans all around you if you allow them to.

Dedicate yourself to the issues that deserve space in your life, or else your life is no different than a million others without agency. Be vigilant about the trials that will propel you ever incrementally toward your chosen ideal. Your actions shape your worldly identity. There is enormous power in choosing what to acknowledge or ignore.

# 23
# Damage and Integration

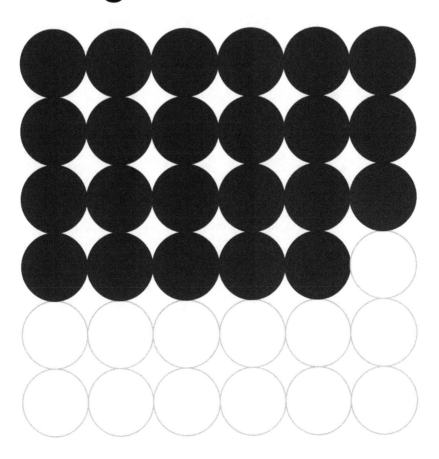

# Damage and Integration

*Under conditions of gradual change, human minds adjust their expectations to the reality created by their thoughts and senses. We guide the flow of our experience toward the states that we prefer, ones congruent with our values and familiar activities. But when changes arrive too swiftly, we might, instead, corrode with longstanding psychological harm. The chaos of the world may grow too complex to process, and we will perceive reality happening, painfully, beyond our permissible territory. If, instead, we can integrate our pain into lessons, we can further our development along our chosen courses.*

◆———————————●———————————◆

For all his power, whether acquired or endowed, a person is always limited to his own arrangement of comfortable operating borders. At or beyond the perimeter of his parameters, he will undergo light or severe personal trauma. Though the pain it brings can carry vital lessons, rushed immersion guarantees the non-integration of those lessons with the whole. Thus, the value depends on patient and meticulous changing of the individual to match his ready awareness to each lesson's needs. Without adaption of the range of acceptable experience, the antiquated structure only seeks out replication of itself in the ideology of its user. Growth then simply ceases.

Everyone's original shared trauma is separation from the womb. The primitive infant has no idea what is happening, only that it wishes to return to the only other state it knows, a state it can never again quite experience. The same qualities continue with damages that occur throughout our lives. Often, they are the result of a sudden change from a safe and comfortable environment to one where everything seems threatening and foreign. The desperate wish in those moments is to run back to the old familiar.

With each new venture into his own damage, a person learns more about his values, limitations, and abilities. But in trying to break a familiar barrier, he may come to spend a great deal of his time recuperating from the ensuing psychic injury. Most crucially, his damage shows him where he is not ready to go because the burden of expansion is too great for him at this time. The residue of fear that damage leaves in its wake is, under ideal conditions, to protect him from self-destruction brought about by careless exploration.

Left to their own methods, minds learn their limits rather quickly. Through tending to their daily needs, they establish patterns and form templates for circumnavigating the discomfort that appears at their boundaries. Such models aid them tremendously at the start but turn perilous when they prohibit genuine expansion. The perpetually expansive person knows that suffering is a necessary companion in his process. He embraces trauma, not as an unfortunate collateral effect, but as the engine to transform himself into more than before. Knowing that suffering is required, he becomes the conductor of his own essential misery.

When we expect reality to show up a certain way, we establish the foundation for our happiness and pain. It is only a matter of time before our expectations cannot be fulfilled completely. In the long run, a life absent major suffering is impossible. None of us can live perfectly prepared for a totally predicted future. No matter the systems of order we build around our comfort requirements, outside events will interfere with them, including even countless unseen elements of latent chaos within them. To live is to endure the harm of unexpected change.

As well, our limitations do not sit forever. They grow or shrink with our behavior. We can sometimes consciously push our minds to be ready for more, driving ourselves by our curiosity and ambition. Alternatively, we may expand the range of our manageable prior damages whenever we become the victims of circumstance, as life arranges itself in such a way that it requires us to act, heroically, beyond what we once knew we could aim for. Then we enter a new kind of landscape, a realm of strange psychological burdens that previously we could not have hoped to carry. Our tolerance for trauma escalates indefinitely alongside us.

Our emotional engagement in reality is what builds our expectations about ephemeral events and is, therefore, the source of all our trauma. Only the experiences we care about hold the capacity to hurt us if they do not go the way we hope them to. Pain is the result of wanting something that we might not be able to acquire or will still be capable of losing even once we do.

We forget that everything material can be lost, and the abrupt annihilation of our attachment to something can scar us for life, conditioning us to re-live the same old injuries without end even long after the loss is complete. We then no longer remember life without the pain that started when our limits suddenly shifted. We cease to expand, and we die in idle repetition, accomplishing nothing for no one anymore. So, it is imperative that we somehow learn to mediate and make meaningful our idle suffering. Our suffering occurs at the pace set only by the depths from which we are capable of recovering.

Always bear in mind the principle that out of countless moments you will experience, only those you interpret as subjectively important will be those that stay with you in the years following their initial occurrence. Understanding in principle what experiences you consider important is the key to understanding, in principle, the nature of your lamentation and, therefore, how to live with it. Some original suffering is certainly necessary for a heroic existence, but you can at least learn to manage it responsibly. You can also learn to leave the unimportant past where it belongs so you will not carry a lifetime of frivolous limitations with you as you go. To do this, you must reassess what you presume you know about your own life.

It is likely you have the type of mind that elects to hold onto old pain because letting go feels like it is killing a vital part of itself. Consequently, your hurt remains because you are afraid to lose something familiar, even if it is something that only brings you pain. It has become so familiar that you have lost sight of who you were without it and, more impactfully, all the other ways you could have and would have grown to be had it not been there.

Realize you're quite a bit more than the deceased past that shaped you. You are the present and all potential futures. You will not lament losing a little part of yourself if its loss clears the way to so much more of you. There is something to be gained from any negative situation if only you can process the damage it generates in you. Perspective can always expand. Appreciation always deepens if you put work into it. You can gain awareness of horrendous events that few others would have had the wherewithal to investigate to the level required.

In the end, the things that have damaged you most can make you kinder, wiser, and nobler than before. Through your kindness, you can protect those not yet as strong as you. Be brave enough to see what harms you as a valuable friend and teacher. When you are ready to take mastery over self-interpretation, your damages will become your adaptations and your pathways to the most heroic version of you.

# 24
# Adaptation and Flow

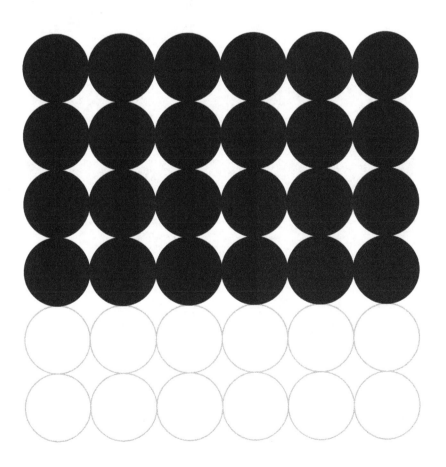

# Adaptation and Flow

*Adaptation is the mechanism by which a mind makes itself better and stronger instead of the opposite in response to unending challenge. As our goal is to master ourselves so we can master our environment, adaptation is how we will equip ourselves to implement our judgment and values in the face of novel obstacles that require our discretion. Given sufficient time and resources, there are no burdens we cannot improve ourselves enough to master. We may even finally begin to realize that the disfunction of the world, which once overran our peace and hope of belonging, can, to some degree, be conquered while we are alive.*

◆———————————————●————————————————●◆

A traveler navigating unknown landscapes, having received false impressions of their layout, will not be able to determine the correct way to his destination. His senses will give him information that contradicts his instructions. But if he were to approach the unknown, assuming nothing beyond what he could directly infer, he would eventually derive the truth through his own experience.

All minds are ignorant of considerable portions of reality and subject to obscurity in their perception. All construct, inherit, and rely on maps never tested for accuracy or completion and enter every situation as facsimiles of reality. All people rely on such cognitive diagrams to maintain the structure of knowledge throughout their evolution.

As no one navigates reality directly, the heuristics they rely on are always incomplete and must adapt with the passage of time and the expansion of perspective. They must flex enough from their original design so that the details align a bit more closely with the truth, or else they will rely on directions that will not actually move them any closer to where they want to go.

Psychological shortcuts are a necessary part of human living. They spare the mind the labor of repetitive analysis so that it need not waste its power on conclusions already arrived at. Applied optimally, they allow the human user to flow with little interruption from one familiar type of trial to another, scarcely even having to think about what he is doing or how he will achieve the resolution he desires. Yet, the possibility of error, even in the familiar, never really dissipates. Variables can change without warning. The mind itself develops defects and hallucinates meaning.

Cognitive clutter is the fog that accumulates in the background of our minds as experience extends indefinitely, preventing us from reacting as we would optimally seek to based on what we encounter in each moment. It makes us biased because we apply the patterns we picked up in the past to situations that do not match them. It is a form of hubris—our presumption that we know everything we need to about even situations we have never encountered. But if we can allow ourselves to forget what we know as soon as it ceases to serve us, we can prevent the fog from building and preserve the clarity of our vision.

Whether or not we actively think about them, our pasts are leashes to our development. We, too often, fail to see that the way things have occurred until now may be irrelevant or arbitrary. So, we must be consciously willing to experience the present anew as a standard aspect of our operation, not merely as an occasional large reset following a major psychological crisis. Our daily maintenance must include the examination of every circumstance as if from nothing, holding zero assumptions about how things go and what's ahead.

So long as there is no real emergency, so long as we are free from immediate concerns to apply our limited thought capacity to, we can instead invest our cognitive resources into laying foundations of new working conceptions of situations that might not conform to how we are used to thinking. But most of us are still too caught up in our stories to reset in such a way. We need to believe that things are how we have believed they are because we don't know any other way to see them, and the burden of deconstructing the orderly perspective we've built is too great. We don't know what emptiness actually feels like. We know only a system of instructions, growing in complexity, telling us what to do and how to feel until the expiration of our lives.

In any new situation you encounter, deduce the changes required to get where you desire. Begin with the simplest modifications you must make to your environment that carry the most substantial impact. What further information will you need to be functional in dealing with what you are now facing? Recognize as quickly as you can when systems work differently than you expect them to so that you will not apply a familiar strategy to an unfamiliar problem. Alter your expectations, one by one, until your internal map fits the new portion of reality as closely as is feasible.

When circumstance requires it, adjust your standards to the minimum necessary amount of expectation by your comfort. Holding only simple ideas about what will happen next makes you more resilient to change and discomfort than depending on a specific series of complex interactions and outcomes. Whenever you have a lot to lose, you are more vulnerable to trauma and discombobulation. With practice, you'll be able to remain calm in the heart of turmoil when your practiced models fail.

In dismantling and remaking your mental models about all things, you will uncover insights that counter what you seem to have previously learned about the laws and systems of the universe. Without the emotional willingness to adapt quite freely, you will become defensive about these changes. Your attachment to your memories will remain your master, and, so long as you have a master, you can never be free to be your full self. Clarity about what is happening and authenticity in your reaction to it only arise when you're not afraid to give up what has incidentally come to define you.

The beauty of releasing preconceptions that no longer (if they ever did) help you navigate the world is that foreign things lose the bulk of their capacity to harm you. Free from these tools turned into restraints, you will resist far less what you do not understand because your first instinct will be to begin crafting new, optimally appropriate tools to deal with it. You will retain the ability to carve out a space for it within your flowing paradigm. All you ever must do in any new situation is deduce what is needed to move from the unprepared person you begin as to a version of yourself who can accomplish what you need from it.

# 25
# Habits and Discoveries

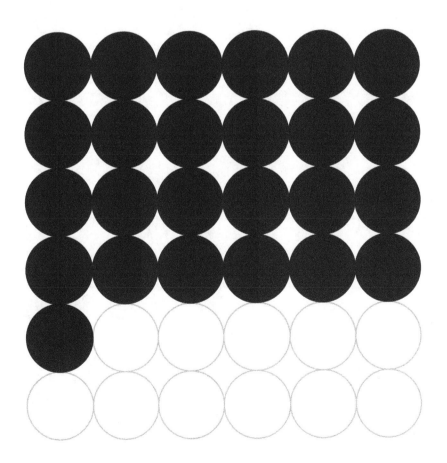

# Habits and Discoveries

*From pure motives comes the discovery of the means to propel away from the collection of unhelpful habits that was present when a journey began. The patterns we encounter before any others, however prohibitive or worthwhile, are never the products of our genuine self-discovery. How could they be? They are, at best, the result of imperfect crafted guidance bestowed on us by our well-intentioned caretakers. At worst, they are the overflow of ubiquitous social commands that give no regard for our personal destinies or ideals. Our task is to examine and eliminate them as needed.*

———————————————————

Principled individuality is the product of a person's applied volition and the visceral feedback he receives from it. Whenever the individual does anything in his life solely due to the pressure to do what he "ought to be doing" by some external worldly standard, he is not living his own life. He is only a reflection of minds more authoritative than his own, minds he could not muster the nerve to overcome. He is submissive to the will of the collective, and his own will all but disappears because of it.

A person without the will to discover everything about himself cannot be heroic. He cannot be true to his own natural ideals because he doesn't yet know who or what he really is. He must clear space for better influence by partaking in fewer of the behaviors that keep him mindlessly busy. He needs to muster the tenacity to pull himself away from cyclical and redundant thoughts that drown his attention, or else he will never be free to cultivate superior concepts for his mind and behaviors for his body. New pastimes will naturally emerge to fill the gaps he has torn inside his previously phony personality.

The exceptional working mind must be able to make reasonable choices about the substance that will occupy its attention and all the ways that it will dedicate its time. But no mind, however gifted, can design its lifestyle until it has undertaken journeys of mythological exploration concerning the intricate and interlocking designs that life can follow. Such simultaneous inner and worldly discovery requires the total use of all one's ambition, intelligence, and acquired self-knowledge, or it will terminate prematurely.

It is not enough for us to limit the extent of our lifestyles to what conventional practices offer to us as possibilities. In order to embody our potential, we ought to be brave enough to adopt new influence that suits our needs wherever we can find it. If we are adaptable and open, we can arrange new experience to complement who we are becoming instead of outright rejecting it because it does not meet what we have been conditioned to tolerate.

But first, we must give up the need for permission from outside authorities who cannot appreciate our nature to organize our lives the way we organically discover is best for us. We must remember that nothing it is physically possible for us to do within this reality is forbidden by any natural standard from occurring. Our permissible limits will be our own to define through our discovery, based only on our developing moral sense of what is right or wrong, correct or incorrect for us to contribute to or partake in. We will not need to restrict ourselves for the sake of another's comfort because our principles will become more important as a result of the arduous process of discovery.

The most important thing we will need to learn is that the advice others pass to us is frequently inappropriate, even if it is well-intentioned. We can still follow the input of society's experts if we see the tangible results of doing so, as weighted by our judgment and values. We can observe the direct effects of the actions they suggest to us. We need only keep these practices so long as we see that they serve us.

Always remember that you will not know what you are capable of evolving into until you give yourself the freedom to figure it out. Every new experience will teach you always a bit more about your unchanging self that has been buried by time and false ideals. In time, your perspective of what you want and can do will escalate as each unique event you wander into opens the way to newer events still. And as your awareness grows, so do your possibilities. You make different choices and establish different patterns for yourself based on what you now realize is true about you and what reality, in all her glory, has to offer.

So, recognize at once that the way you have lived your life and spent the bulk of your available time until now may have been largely meaningless as it regards your mythological development. Much has probably been wasted in spinning your wheels with empty distraction, if not actively pushing you away from the fully realized hero character you believe you are destined to become. You do not need to follow the examples set by others around you any longer.

Specific actions and the obvious products that result from them are not what are essential to the final analysis regarding your development. The impact of what you do will be personally profound if you act in the right emotional state and for the right reasons. Meaningful development happens when you witness the outcomes of your behavior. Your evaluation of the consequences is what spurs your burgeoning growth. So, even if there is no evident and tangible result from the hobbies that occupy your waking time, there may still be profound structural changes happening beneath your visible surfaces.

When you adopt new lifestyle habits not because they are expected of you but because they help incarnate your deepest desires, you design your life after your own image for the first time. Finally, you need not permission to move in any new direction that supports your ambitions, only the realization that the choice brings you closer to a state more genuinely fulfilling than the one you knew before. The world is full of assets to assimilate into the structure of you. You only need to make sure that you never allow yourself to get trapped in an attractive but limiting pattern along the way.

# 26
# Narrative
# and Bias

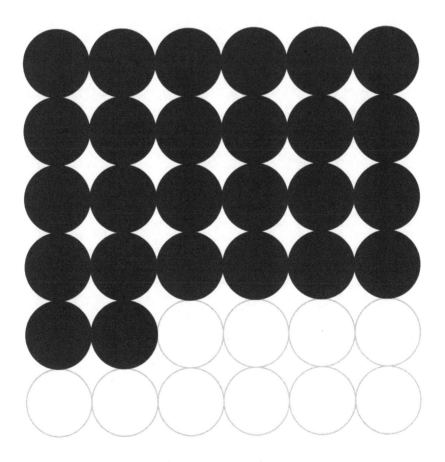

# Narrative and Bias

*Conception is neither static nor complete. The whole of reality can be pulled apart and arranged into structures that happen to support our momentary wants, regardless of how they might belie our values. Our paths turn mythological when their narrative changes activate the deepest, unchanging elements of our designs. For this to happen, we must remain steadfast and committed to clarity, especially when it would be far easier to obscure our view with convenient layers of illusion.*

———◆———

Reality cannot be taken as a whole. It should be picked apart to be comprehended. As any mind is biased, it focuses on the patterns and pieces that stand out to it as more important than the rest. These, it believes, it can arrange into useful structures to comprehend and act upon. It sees what appears to help it accomplish the tasks it considers worthwhile. In fact, it sees only what matters to its goals, which themselves are arbitrary and ever-changing.

From the details of apparent importance that stand out first, the mind constructs narratives to contain the entire meaning of its experience. It relies on the stories it writes or that others have written for it to make sense of the endless streams of detail it encounters. Narrative creates its structure, and even a faulty or incomplete structure seems better than none at all in the moment of analysis. Thus, all people become entrapped by the biases of their minds and their cultures and the filtering effect they have upon the feed of raw experience they share.

Any narrative, however endearing or useful, is only a framework of subjective meaning. Through it, all life's micro-adventures contribute to a broader purpose that defines the perceiver. The people of Earth, finding great difficulty in determining their own narratives of importance without instruction, cannot order reality into structures that aid and expand their sense of purpose. Without purpose, an unordinary life can never rise above the rest. A life without an original and authentic narrative of meaning goes on only for the sake of going on, to perpetuate the patterns it adopts from its cultural environment.

A gifted introspector, one who pays special attention to how his mind arranges reality into meaningful forms, can step away from the stories he tells himself about what it all is supposed to mean and where his attention ought to go. With space and self-reflection, he can choose new ways to narrate the events of his life. The whole meaning of his reality can be remade in an instant without ever once contradicting the facts of what has occurred, all because he has opted for a new position and lens to view it from. In the end, the narrative is just what he is noticing, the selective truth of his limited individual awareness.

Without a narrative structure that facilitates our evolution as protagonists, our story repeats without end. We solve the same problems time and again until we are dead. Without a story to tie everything together, our lives become chaos absent order. Progress becomes impossible because we have no way to measure how close we are to our goals. We do not even know where we are going or where we are in relation to it. We have no means by which to determine the significance of what we have done until now or what we must do next. But with narrative, we can embrace the lessons of the trials we overcome and change on an intimate level through them.

On the timeless path of the hero, we move as efficiently as we can from one trial to the next. We take what we are ready for as soon as we are ready. Our problems and rewards escalate at the rate we can accommodate them. Leaving the comfort of home to conquer the unfamiliar, we expand the boundaries of our home territory and beget for ourselves new forms of creative meaning. All genuine personal development holds to this model at its core.

When we recognize that we have been paying attention to what outside forces dictated for us instead of building filters to our perception based on our own values, we break away from their erroneous narration and write stories of our own. We may assign the purpose and meaning that will grant to us a sense of victory as we define it. However we construct them, the biases we let remain in our minds must somehow serve to move us toward righteousness and further from submission to entropy.

Hero myths persist across the generations because they speak to your inherent potential to evolve, to break out of persistent cycles, and to ascend to ones of higher existential value where you may finally find the fulfillment whose lack has burdened you for as long as you remember. The consequence of understanding this is realizing that you are never just living one life but many lives in sequence. It is up to you to identify where you are in the process and for what purpose you allow it to repeat once more.

A new story begins with each new problem that arises in your awareness. From comfort, you enter discomfort. You remain there until it becomes a regular part of your identity. Then, you wander forward yet again until you encounter still another problem to occupy you. The myth is cyclical, escalating in scope with each return to the known start. You should seek to always recognize where you are in the cycle. When one plot reaches its resolution, the onset of another is sure to follow.

No matter what the world is telling you to put your attention into, you are free to set your own vision and write your own stories. When you cease to fill your time with repetitive dramas, you can focus on the principle of your arc. The recurring themes in your life show you what to look for. The repeated conflicts you run into are the weaknesses you have yet to integrate into your patterned understanding. Your antagonists are the people who represent the opposite of what you stand for. Your dragons are whatever great injustices you cannot allow to continue so long as you have the strength to oppose them. These pillars define the course your many lives will take. They light the way for what is yet to come for the time you have left in the world.

# 27
# Earnestness and Confidence

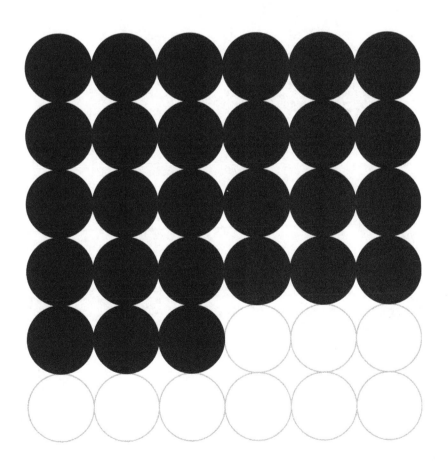

# Earnestness and Confidence

*Without earned and accurate self-confidence in actions taken and paths chosen, the noblest of aims will be, by requisite, misguided. We inevitably end up moving toward the wrong ends or simply moving in the wrong ways toward the right ones. Our minds develop the habit of sabotaging themselves before ever attaining anything remotely worthwhile according to the metrics we have narrowly arrived at through deep inner examination. Our earnest self-confidence derives from what we have seen we can accomplish under duress and the durability of the mythic lens through which we view our roles in the world.*

———————◆———————

It takes a masterful amount of grit and fortitude to find a way out of the containers of a faulty inherited self. Trying to do so without complete confidence in the authenticity of the persona underneath makes it too easy to fall back into the comfortable and illusory shell of the person inhabiting it. The further one strays from what he has grown accustomed to seeing himself and encouraging the world to treat him as, the more lost he will feel. Earned self-confidence is what makes the wandering process bearable.

Self-knowledge is the foundation for all other knowledge because the self is what interprets all else. The further someone's conception of self strays from the objective truth of the matter, the less power he has to live as himself and rely on how he sees the world. His priority should be to know the intimate nature of his own identity before literally anything else, as it is necessarily antecedent. Every lingering question about who he is underneath the facade must be stamped out at once, or he is sure to fail before he begins.

As the way he sees himself influences everything else about him, it is really the individual's meta-awareness that defines who he is more than anything else. But this inwardly pointed awareness requires tremendous accuracy to be useful, or else it will end up being the very opposite. If he can manage to conceptualize himself as he really is, his feelings, thoughts, and actions won't be likely to wander into self-indulgent fantasy that, while providing a temporary sense of completion, only take him further out of reality. He must first know who he is in order to live his life accordingly

Confidence necessarily stems from our opinions of ourselves. The benefits of confidence do not come from believing all things possible but from believing in our ability to improve. To be effective, we have to trust our ability to adapt to whatever challenges confront us, and this belief is the product of being intimately familiar with our capabilities and limitations. The process of discovering ever more about ourselves as we age and explore is our most significant source of power.

Sometimes, we may, in inspired moments, set goals for ourselves that rest far outside our present comfort. But then, as we begin to approach them, the false idea of who we are and what we can do stops us by reminding us who we think we ought to be. This lack of confidence keeps us tethered to one station, never straying too far from where it insists that we belong. The false self becomes the master, and the true self dies before it ever has the chance to show.

A lack of personal confidence is just another out of countless forms of self-delusion imposed on us to keep us easier to control. When we reach alignment between the objective truth of what we are and what we subjectively conceive ourselves to be, confidence becomes our natural state. And then, when we are fully confident, we experience more of ourselves because we are more active. We are empowered to perform a broader range of tasks and utilize more of the characteristics that make us who we are. As self-confident people not tied to any one mode of being, we move in any direction we set our sights to and, ultimately, activate everything we are capable of.

Confidence, if it is truly earned, is highly selective in its application. Arrogance, though appearing similar to the unaware, is unearned. Arrogance does not discriminate as it should. Arrogance claims contradictory things simultaneously, never hesitating or reflecting about its place in the identity. Confidence holds that what is true is true, and what is possible is possible. It knows what it can accomplish and earns its reward. Arrogance prefers to jump ahead to an unearned pseudo-victory. You, having earned your self-confidence, can restructure your psyche, reshape your body, and learn tools as necessary to channel your influence into the areas of life you care about.

Before you take on any significant tasks in your pursuit of heroic meaning, make it your priority to match your perception of yourself to the reality of you. Strip away faulty filters about what you mean to the world and yourself. Hold onto who you know yourself to be as you make your way in the process of evolving. Believe with all your mind that what is true is true because you have uncovered it to be so through your exploration of yourself. To progress beyond the point of what you can genuinely know about yourself through tests and trials is pompous. You only earn certainty in your opinions about yourself when you have checked them against the cold hard truth.

Real confidence is attainable when you are willing to abandon old perceptions in a moment because truth becomes more critical to you than favorable pretense. Anything else is a gratifying delusion. Wherever the truth about you ends up being, there should be your goal. Only whatever is real is your ally. That ally, once adopted, becomes an incredibly potent tool for both staying true to your principles when it is inconvenient and dismantling the greatest barriers standing between where you are and what you want. Accepting both your weaknesses and your strengths is the smartest thing you could do in pursuit of a life that holds both comfort and purpose, a dichotomy oft thought incompatible by those who fall too far into one end of either loving or hating themselves too much.

# 28
# Arrogance
# and Elevation

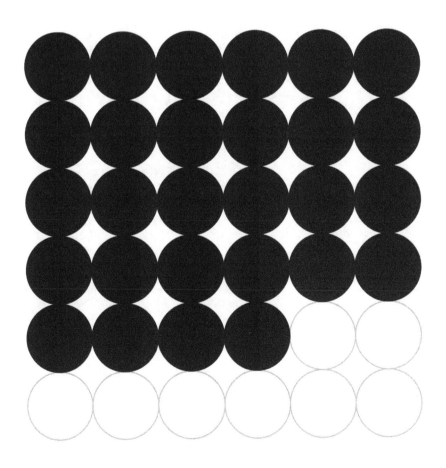

# Arrogance and Elevation

*Confidence and self-esteem, if they are meaningful, arrive via commitment to great problems and difficulties to be conquered. Alternatively, accepting any premature and arbitrary sense of importance just because it alleviates our discomfort without exposing us to the necessary struggle, risk, and investment only taints our perception of self. We must work to keep our pride in check and our projections grounded, or we will quickly lose our focus on reality. If we build our identities on erroneous foundations, the path will only take us further from our values and our destinies.*

———————————————

It is necessary for survival that at some point early in development, all people begin to think themselves special, unique, and somehow distinct from the whole of reality. An ordinary human life plays out in a series of attempts to uphold an inflated sense of self, driven by fear of obsolescence to the society on which he depends. The impossible standard can never be satisfied, and the host remains unfulfilled until he dies.

A mind obsessed with self-importance desires unrealistic things to be real about itself, but merely wishing them so does never makes them so. Even pretending that they are true, which the world easily mistakes for genuine self-confidence, does not make them any more likely to become magically real. In fact, persisting in self-delusion too long will only birth more impossible and inauthentic standards for the self. Such a deluded mind remains segregated from the shared and objective universe around it, to the point that it loses any reliable reference for what is true. By then, it may be lost irreversibly to its own self-aggrandizing delusions.

Any imaginings of one's own development are no more real than daydreams or fairy tales unless reality allows for them to become real through appropriate actions. But a person who believes too highly in his own importance quickly forgets this. He unconsciously accepts that he has special permission to act in ways that others do not, for no other reason than that he is himself and others are not. Such is the soul of arrogance.

The self-important person, whatever his actual gifts or merits, develops the habit of positioning himself exclusively above the world and never among it. More than that, the mechanisms and justifications by which he elevates himself can never be countered. He proclaims his position unassailable. As factual reality is not enough for him, he inflates himself to seem like something more than what he could ever achieve through heroic principle and action. He presumes invincibility to compensate for insecurity. Only the genuinely humble person, who has seen himself fall, split apart at the seams, and dissected into his base components, knows that no matter what exceptional traits he holds, he is always subject to the same rules as the universe.

Projected self-certainty is a cheap and, ultimately, ineffectual means to empowerment. Pretending to be something we are not is guaranteed to be unsustainable. Confidence compensations will always fade because they have

155

no root in reality. Under their illusion, we will always find ourselves return-
ing to the groundless place where we began, ever afraid to lose the fleeting
feeling of false power once we have acquired it.

No matter how much we may wish it, no amount of pretense could ever
change the truth of who and what we are as individuals. So long as we are
afraid to lose the elevated fantasy we have imagined for ourselves, our stunt-
ed minds look exclusively outside themselves for the causes of our suffering. If we never blame ourselves for our misfortune, we remain in a state
of chronic victimhood to life's inherent unfairness and mistreatment. Our
victim minds see improvement as unnecessary, and we cannot change the
flaws we don't acknowledge.

Under the influence of arrogance, we cease to interact with the world and
deal only with ourselves. To us, life is unfair when it does not coincide with
our prescription for how it should go, and everyone is an enemy who does
not immediately affirm the story we put out for others to adopt about us.
Other people are the causes of all our suffering because we cannot let go of
our position of rightness in our minds, no matter how contrived or inconsis-
tent our reasoning must become to hold to it in all circumstances.

Real confidence results only from accurate conceptions of who we are. Arrogance exists far beyond accuracy, distorting the truth to match our insecurities. We do not earn excellence by assigning idle importance to ourselves.
Excellence arrives from altering ourselves to embody the standards we de-
mand from all reality. But if we remain arrogant, we will be frightened by
the possibility of not even being good enough to meet our own standards.
We will always be seeking to redefine success to be whatever we already have
accomplished and attributed to ourselves. Whatever we do is what should
be done. Whatever we say is true becomes the truth because we are the ones
who have said it. We have become our own false gods.

To humble yourself from a state of perpetual arrogance is to willfully lower
your life to the same playing field as all else in existence that must abide by
the same earthly rules. It is to realize there are no special permissions that
apply only to you, at least none that do not have to be earned through will
and action. You are still a functioning sub-component of universal law and
principle. You are not important solely by birthright, no matter how different your nature seems to be from the ordinary substance all around you. All
that the circumstances of your birth can ever grant you is potential, but your
destiny is yours alone to see completed.

The test of a consistent worldview is whether internal analysis wars with outside observations or the two meet in mutual agreement. Learn to look upon
yourself as you look upon others. Do not pick out only the best elements
of your existence to pay attention to and disregard the rest. You need both
deep appreciation and carefully constructed criticism in order to fully evolve.

When you look upon yourself, what is truly remarkable or worthwhile? How
do you see yourself without the bias of unearned confidence? Instead of assuming that your excellence must be within you by default, seek to earn it by

your actions. Work to become exceptional in a manner you can be proud of for the duration you are alive. Strive to adopt the qualities for yourself that you admire so much in others to be worthy of your own admiration.

With time, you'll see that even though you may have been born exceptional by natural accidents outside your control, genuine excellence comes from the choices you make about what to do with your endowments. If you overlook your part in making conscious choices about how you will act, you place yourself strictly above your fellow man. You exclude yourself from the laws of human behavior and from dealing with the consequences of your choice. As such, you construct an ironic sort of cage for your growth out of your elevated ego, and you forfeit your ability to learn, grow, and evolve into something forever more heroic.

# 29
## Cripplement
## and Sabotage

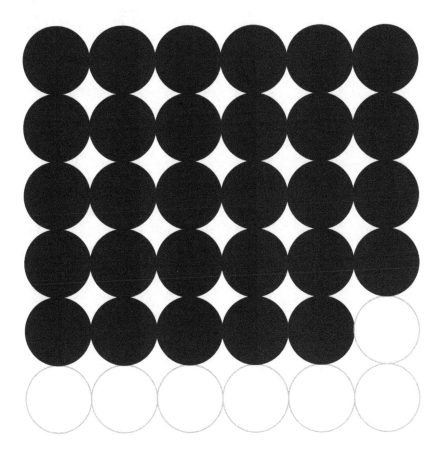

# Cripplement and Sabotage

*No matter the potential that exists, if, in the process of development, should no weight be placed into the identity that is developing and the roles sought to be played, all success will be undermined before there is even a genuine chance to fail. To lack confidence in our own importance is to enable a thousand false values to flood in our awareness, drawing our attention where we do not wish for it to go. So long as we remain crippled by unwillingness to see what has been proven to be real, we will remain mostly useless for the goals we see as necessary to our sanity and purpose.*

---

The accurate acknowledgment of objective truths and virtues pertaining to oneself is a crucial part of living up to one's potential. Pathological doubts twist the perception of reality to make it constrictive and demeaning. Any positive interpretations get undermined by undue negative feelings festering just outside of conscious understanding. These self-destructive feelings become the new foundation for every belief and, ultimately, a person's worldview as a whole.

One who cannot endorse with his emotions what he cognitively knows as credible cannot embody his accumulated self-knowledge with his actions. He will never completely accept that he is deserving of the virtue and moral development that he seeks for his life, even when he is already nearly there. Until he has the fortitude to act on what he knows, his worldly development is on hold.

If he blames his absent progress on externalities or conjured-up illusions about his limitations, he will never look inside himself to find the real source of his stagnation. He will never rectify the inner nature of his sabotage, the cause that leaks through to all he does. He will not permit himself to suture the wounds that first caused him to disconnect from a realistic conception of what he can do because it hurts to even look at them. He will ignore the systemic source of his repeated pain and trauma, obsessing over details that do not matter to the cause.

If he remains the type of person who does not make his development his highest priority, he will accomplish nothing of lasting significance for himself, the people he cares about, or the principles that are supposed to shape him. Instead, all his actions become paltry attempts to fill the lack within himself. The hole has to be plugged, or meaningful development dies before it settles. Nothing positive accumulates without the truth as its foundation.

Self-sabotaging ideas can be so disastrous to heroism because they are cumulative by nature. They grow in us over the long-term experience of our lives, rarely shrinking or disappearing of their own accord. Many of us quietly become conditioned to believe that pride of any kind is unforgivable and that we are practically demonic to think even a little too highly of ourselves. We learn that it is only the humblest of women and men, the meekest and most self-deprecating, who are deserving of moral praise and association with virtue.

The primary reason we fear judgment from others is that, ironically, we judge ourselves more harshly than they ever could. We do not accept who we are, and we fear that no one else can either. But the confident versions of us who base their self-perception in provable values and assertions care not about these opinions. When we know who we are, beyond doubt, it will not matter the slightest amount what the rest of the world thinks about us. Outside condescension only matters if it reflects our own opinions, if it is of such a form that it can slip into the cracks in the armor we've constructed to protect our vulnerable innards. Only what amplifies our insecurities can hurt us.

However, as we grow braver, we can begin to recognize the importance of overcoming our hesitations about our nature and abilities. We can confront every doubt and every dread, every fear that has curtailed our ambition until now and prevented us from achieving the existence we have long suspected we are capable of and, under ideal developmental conditions, destined to embody. We can critically examine and manipulate the part of ourselves that undeservingly condemns our aspirations and rejects the heroic responsibility of our potential.

Do not expect immediate social validation when you make the choice to move away from crippling and habitual self-sabotage. Those in your life who have not mastered themselves will always feel a need to place you into categories that affirm the stories they tell themselves about their own presumed importance, their own invented place in the world. The upholding of their sense of false identity requires the subjugation of your real one. Do not diminish the truth about yourself to bolster the fantasy of another.

When you accept who you are, you won't care much at all what the world thinks of you. You will hardly even consider their opinions with a sober mind, except as an exercise in empathy and enhanced perspective. The truth you will have learned to inwardly narrate about yourself, the one that emanates from familiarity and integration of the principles that shape you, will be vastly more important than any seeds of doubt once cast upon you by voices external.

Although eliminating self-doubt does not make you invincible to attack, it grants you a far more accurate and useful platform from which to operate in the world, from which to live out the virtue of your principles more fully. Even without internal sabotage, you will still face challenges. You will still fight difficult battles that maim and tarnish. You will still fail and find injury that inhibits your ability to carry out your sacred tasks. You may even die. But you'll be more prepared to do so with your head held high, knowing that you lived the best you could and were not afraid to know yourself or pursue your ideals.

Furthermore, you'll believe in your ability to learn from every hardship because you'll have the experience necessary to have seen yourself do so. You'll know that sacrifices are worthwhile because they stimulate your growth and allow you to meditate upon your choices and values. Struggle will no longer intimidate you because it will have been struggle that has molded you. You will appreciate every victory, and you will have learned what it means to accept the nature of what you are.

# 30
## Control
## and Chaos

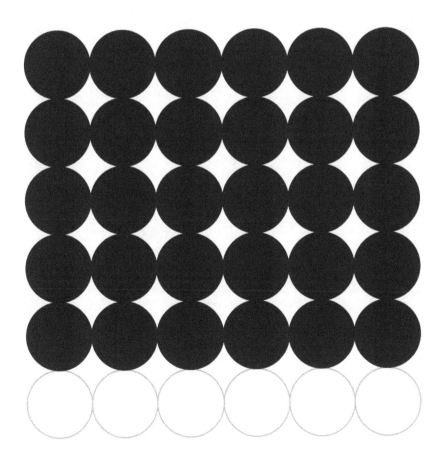

# Control and Chaos

*Choices are made in every moment that either push the world into or pull it from its structureless disorder. To choose the path of order and virtue requires us to rise above the natural inclination toward chaos because it appears a faster and easier means to the emotional resolution we desire. When we can do this on a daily basis with our ordinary emotions, we can begin to act heroically on a grander social level. But the ability to make such a choice depends upon us first knowing and acknowledging what darkness we are capable of so that we might keep it in check before it comes to overwhelm us.*

———————————————————

Good is the force that shields structure from disruption and guards curated order. Anything that tears a system apart or extracts parts from its whole for incompatible purposes is chaos, and if it is done with the conscious intention of harming the people who protect that order by pushing them into entropy, it is malevolent evil. A good person sees his life as a critical component of a larger whole that he has identified as more important to him. He is a sub-component of a greater system, a living sub-portion of his total reality. His task is to scale the influence of his principles throughout his system to the best of his ability.

The sacrifice of short-term needs and superficial priorities comes easily to a good person because he knows he is not actually losing himself when he forsakes his immediate happiness to maintain the order of the systems he commits to. He is not eliminating himself but, rather, expanding himself exponentially whenever he suffers a loss in service to his values. His permanent sense of purpose arrives by investing his identity into something more important than his temporary comforts.

But while structure is necessary for good, preoccupation with order will stifle its optimal development and sustainable arrangement. The too-comfortable mind sees nearly any change beyond what it has grown used to as evil and unwelcome. It resists deconstruction because it assumes that things are the best that they can be. It hardly ever considers that the way it does things may have been flawed from the start and require total reconsideration for the sake of the aims that it seeks.

Chaos is attractive when it resolves immediate needs. But such a perspective requires the individual to disregard the order of the systems all around him. Chaos limits its worldview to only momentary concerns and stimuli, not the holistic view that leads to a fairer long-term interpretation. Its disposition lies in instantaneous gratification. Chaotic actors have no interest in the downstream repercussions of their plans, no holistic perspective from which to evaluate the merit of their choices. They eliminate systemic order for personal gain. A pathological villain is merely a person who has adopted disorder as his primary motivator. He destructs for the sake of destruction. The villainous actor has identified far too completely with his unresolvable emotions.

There is a prominent lie that, in order to be good people, we must identify unambiguously with only the positive half of two opposing forces that compose our inescapable nature, each forever battling the other for dominance and control over our personalities. But the outright denial of our darkness is as erroneous as our submission to it. Denial only pushes it from conscious view and makes us superficially good because we lack the perspective to understand our capacity for monstrosity and destruction.

If we are only good by default, we fear what we will find when we look within and, for the first time, uncover our inclination for selfish gain at the expense of our surroundings. That fear of what we could do or become will limit our capacity to act from our better parts, limiting our influence. Even the "good" hero must recognize when destruction is required, and he must, at times, act destructively with full awareness of the nature and purpose of what he does, neither succumbing to lust and rage nor losing control in any other way that is associated with true evil.

What we need is a healthy integration of our warring dynamics. We need every part of ourselves in its rightful place, applied for its most appropriate conditions and nothing more. A true and complete hero, which is what we should strive to be, considers the collateral effects of all his efforts. He does not ever become single-minded such that he allows himself to hyper-focus on his objective and ignore the removed effects of his behavior, for it is impossible to do anything of substance without cascading externalities. That is our responsibility and burden.

We will always be tempted, in some form, to overlook the extensions of our values and the structures of our goals. Narrow, consuming greed can always divert us from the path. Obsession with any particular sort of stimulation might cause us to forget the meaning of what we build. Lust can arise for any sort of sensory pleasure, transmuting our virtue into vice. We should all beware our momentary desires, for they can betray us if we do not grant them the credit they deserve. When an instinctual attraction causes the abandonment of hard-won order, we let our inner chaos commandeer our higher-order chosen principles.

Every aspect of your identity has a place and a context to surface. Every part can recede when your environment does not need it any longer. You have nothing to fear about expressing questionable parts of yourself so long as you keep your motivation in place when the destruction of something stagnant or actively harmful is actually needed. How will you respond when a controlled form of chaos is the only solution? Even chaos in service of order?

For a mature and open mind, there are no concepts so terrible as to be forbidden from consideration. The mere assessment of your own potentiality should not incapacitate you. Have you not ever wondered if you were capable of what you consider to be the lowest abyss of human behavior? That if the capacity existed in you to do the awful things you associate with history's greatest monsters and the most deranged of human minds? Or have you only instantly shunned such thoughts from your mind, fearing what you might become if you allowed your curiosity to even wander?

GREGORY V. DIEHL

The way to neutralize the harm of chaotic desires is to analyze, understand, and integrate them into the personality you aspire to embody. Your only choice is to reach a level of intimacy with yourself such that no cavity or capacity is left unsearched, and no dark surprises lie in waiting to disrupt you from your path. Acknowledge your so-called darker side for what it is and realize there are valid reasons for it. Do you still remain virtuous once you allow your mind to wander to where it should not be allowed to go? Or do you become impelled to participate in forbidden sins?

Whatever rules you in your imagination is your master in reality too. The part of you that you cannot integrate is the real-world devil from which all folklore takes its influence. If you think you have no monstrous side, you are living as only half a person. It is better to master your darkness while you are young than to hide it away until it has grown out of your control. Remember that everything existing inside you is just a piece of your totality. You don't have to fear any part of it if you are prepared to manage it and apply it responsibly.

# 31
# Method and Structure

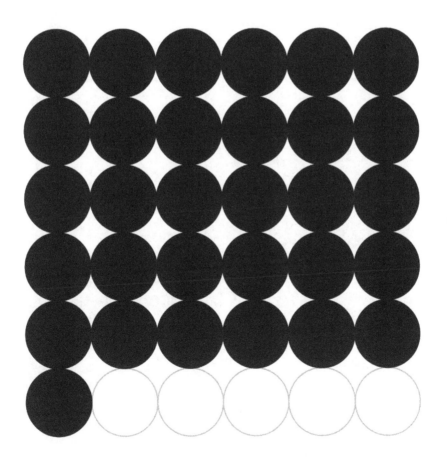

# Method and Structure

*A mind selects its priorities from among infinite alternative possibilities in any situation. From them, we maintain our operating order for the world as we happen to perceive it. Our structure is our spotlight in obscurity, enabling us to focus on what matters to our desires and filter out intruding thoughts, feelings, and stimuli that do not serve our values. Through the structure it bestows on us, we come to identify entirely with the pursuit of meaningful tasks, so long as we can bypass the abundant incoming chaos that would dislodge us from our paths. We alone choose what, out of the infinite, is worthy of considering and keeping and what serves our sacred values.*

---

It is a great and lengthy undertaking to discover what one values most in life. It is even greater to pursue it without having to fight oneself about every little detail concerning the pursuit or growing paralyzed with fear of failure along the way. No matter what a person thinks is most important to him, there are countless other avenues that might satiate momentary wants and cause him to neglect the deeper sense of purpose that his priorities should be granting.

Each new generation, having greater options for entertainment or distraction than all that came before it, faces the heaviest burden yet. Theirs is a greater challenge to select, from among the many, those thoughts and activities that will add momentum to their values or detract it from them. Opportunities expand with time, and with them come expanded responsibilities. So long as novelty constantly emerges in the mind, there can be no clarity in the choices it commits to. Prioritization becomes a necessity so that the purposeful mind can elect what it will allow to surface inside.

Surface distractions often only come to dominate if a person needs them to cover the deeper pain of his unfulfilled desires. They pull a mind's attention away from conscious goals because the weight of awareness about an important and unfinished task is too much for most to handle. Because there is always an abundance of ideas about potentialities, normal minds are rather unable to decide what is most integral to their stated ideal and what they ought to do first. There are no absolute or even reliable means by which to segregate the mass according to one's consciously chosen values. Discretion is the key.

A mature mind is one that has learned to bridle the flow forcefully entering it from every direction. The delicate cognitive framework, once an important task is decided, must be nurtured. However, the modern world is infinitely nuanced, evolving, and always entertaining to curious and excitable minds. It can easily distract us from our chosen purpose and pursuits. Though experience helps the mind to grow, it can fall into cycles of repeating the same stimuli or excitements well beyond the point that they are contributing to its development. When that happens, its growth begins to fester.

A thousand streams of information move into our minds every day we are alive. Each of us contributes a personal bit of conflict to the collective intangible struggle. Ideas and activities compete for our finite ability to process them. We should not be so quick to yield to them but, instead, maintain control over which, out of all possible activities, will be the ones we engage in via our senses and decisions. Despite our chronic growing in experience, most of us simply relive the same lessons under only superficially different worldly encounters. The distractions of ordinary life keep us stagnant in the search for quick solutions to our discontentment through rapid bursts of meaningless stimulation, never going deeper into our pain or motivation to discover more of the structure that defines us.

It is our duty to ourselves to ensure, to the best of our abilities, that as many of the pursuits we fill our time with as possible, in some subjectively meaningful manner, contribute to the state of operation we desire to hold in the world. The problem with distractions that are not rightful priorities in our lives is that they only serve to make us feel better about our experience of living. They do not help us become the things we foresee ourselves to be capable of being. They offer only reward and no risk or investment. And if we do not have to fear losing anything that we consider worth keeping in our lives, we do not grant our choices the weight that they should carry.

There will always be sensory needs our animal minds compel us to try to satisfy the quickest ways we know. The human experience is full of itches that need scratching. It is unavoidable. We all feel bored, lacking in arousal, and, from time to time, a deep and persistent need to indulge in immediate pleasure and pull our attention away from longstanding stresses or inadequacies. While there is nothing inherently unhealthy about the temptation for self-satisfaction, empty pleasures do not serve our heroic development. What we really need are pleasures that carry enough personal responsibility that they require us to grow as we simultaneously satisfy our pressing desires. Shallow indulgence is the problem.

Recall the dread that came upon you when you first realized that ordinary pursuits would not provide any meaningful form of lasting satisfaction for you. You began then to know then that you wanted more than a life of insignificant distraction or relationships and identification from simple pastimes. And still, until now, this knowledge has haunted you because you have not figured out a reliable way to structure your life around the grander pursuits you know you are drawn to. That pain has seeped into your core. It binds you to your path, offering you strength and focus when distraction is too strong, giving you power not to yield to chronic stimuli.

You will, however, always, still indulge, to some degree, in the world's unending busy pleasures, but your nature will make you grow dissatisfied by them all the more quickly and easily. You will know it right away when some novelty has shown you the limits of its value within your developing structure. You will see when you have reached the limits of what any new form of entertainment can offer you. You will take what you can from that experience and move to whatever comes next, never yielding to any easy, instantly entertaining but ultimately shallow hobby. The task is to find that exceptional minority of recreations that is sustainably both entertaining and meaningful for you, which will free up your discretion to focus on the mythic changes you seek to make in the world.

So, move along when you recognize that childish pursuits no longer serve you. Focus on something more. Go so deep into unhappiness that you destroy your comfortable and familiar patterns. In uncomfortable emptiness, your mind will automatically start to crave the same excitements it knows from a thousand times before. But it will only act this way for a time. When you become the master of your interest, your curiosity will serve your values throughout your life. You will decline, at will, those trivial pursuits that don't contribute to your ultimate destination. And you will come to find all the more entertaining whatever it is that actually adds to your existential development, regardless of the social categories those activities conventionally belong to. You master both yourself and your reality when it is you, alone, that attributes labels, categories, and relevance to all you ever do.

# 32
# Disruption and Revolution

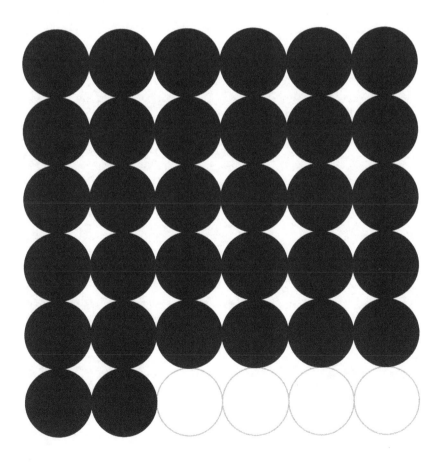

# Disruption and Revolution

*Heroic potential is only eventually reached by the placement of mythological development as the highest of all priorities, but it often only comes at the interim cost of sensory comfort and societal cohesion. We cannot remain too comfortable too long, or our impressive ambition quickly atrophies. So, it is imperative that we seek out the opportunity to dislodge ourselves from intermittent states of mediocrity we settle into, no matter how bitter doing so might make us feel. If we do not consciously move into disruption when circumstance calls for it, we will soon forget the importance of our missions and the original great disappointment that moved us onto them.*

◆———————————————◆

The sensitive and perceptive portion of the population cannot ever come to solve the problems inherent to their existence so long as they feel coerced to operate at the level of their peers, for their peers will work only within known and conventional capacities. For heightened people, suffering persists if they squander their potential for profundity by avoiding challenge or examination, always placing comfort as the highest priority. Any deviation from the default must be corrected before it can pivot any further, or else the rogue pilot risks going so far beyond acceptable limits that he can never return.

The lifestyles these people know, their present identities, are defined by the predictable and recurring stimuli that produce the thoughts, actions, and emotions they claim as their own. The only way these patterns ever change is through interruption in a meaningful sort of way so that they may be replaced by something more directly connected to the owner's ideal role in the universe. But will that necessary interruption come by force from afar or by voluntary tampering within?

Any who fear the depths of their own nature will never have the chance to know the restructuring that stems out of tactical deconstruction. Without the will to disrupt, the natural inclination is to stick with whatever a person already believes about who he is, what the world allowed him to express about himself as he matured within it, and nothing more. Humanity tends to perpetuate the behaviors it knows will work and receive acceptance in the conditions that have, from its perspective, determined its survival. It has a strong inherent interest in retarding unexpected growth so that no individual's progress can exceed its boundaries.

So long as the recurring elements of life have been derived from half-truth, illusion, and the carried-over inefficiencies of generations prior, it remains impossible to learn of one's true destiny or values. And so, the exceptions operating outside the rule have little chance to develop the necessary bravery or ambition to embody themselves until they embrace total inquiry about the nature and path of their development. Only intentional self-disruption can dislodge them from the counterfeit lives the conventional world has reared them into.

177

Our self-fulfilling worldly paths may be so familiar to us now that we never even notice their constricting influence on our trajectories. We might think we know how and why we behave the ways we do, but the reasons we know are only those the world has given us permission to apply in shallow examination. That is the real danger: to delude ourselves into thinking we have made real choices and performed thorough analyses when we obviously have not. So long as we are at least a little discontent, we still have hope for breakthrough.

We know before we begin that uprooting familiar structures will leave us afloat in idle strangeness. The pain of our disruption must be strong enough to dislodge us from where we have previously settled. As our bodies undergo new types of strain, our minds can elevate to higher operation to compensate for the pain. The discomfort of our expansion can be endured this way. It not, we will not garner anything meaningful and permanent for our internal schematics, and our trauma will be meaningless.

Sometimes, it requires only a lone catalyst to lead to an escalation of disruptive revolutions, radically altering our paths. Whatever most challenges the erroneous premises at the center of our illusions has the greatest potential to pivot the trajectories of our lives. But though the inciting disruptive incident may be random or accidental, the cascading influence can be shaped by our awareness of what we need to learn from it.

The more we reflect on where we are and what has brought us to where we currently rest, the easier it becomes to undo those causes and improve them. Once we remove the internal need for early reference points, we will feel the pull to venture into places that once would have been far outside our reach while we were still shackled to familiarity. If we see that things that once satisfied us no longer do, we will have nowhere to go but into the deep unknown.

The world as you know it will not likely support you in your changes. It won't even know how to categorize you, so it may shun you the way it does with everything it does not have a place for. Unless you learn to present yourself in a way they can approve, you will remain a frightening potentiality that serves to remind them there is more than they are willing to consider. The beginning of disruption, after all, is just knowing that you don't want any more what the world chose for you. The contrarian impulse is, at first, enough to dislodge you from its formula, but it is not enough to sustain your trajectory or grant genuine personal meaning to your path. The resolution to an unfulfilling life does not lie in rooting down further into it but in disrupting old patterns of activity with forethought and intention.

You will always have an incomplete understanding of what is going on in you and where you are going. With each disruption come new opportunities, outcomes, and events you could never have foreseen. In fact, that is a major part of the point of disruption. Progress arrives most readily when excruciating self-reflection causes you to see that the way you have built your life until now is incompatible with what you suspect you might or should become. However, the older you get, the more of yourself you will have invested into your recurring structure. Therefore, the more powerful your disruption will need to be.

You will always reach plateaus in your development as you wander. Learn what you can from these intermittently stable periods, and then disrupt them deliberately so that you may ascend to something greater. There is always something worthy of deconstruction or undoing within you, even when all seems well on your path. Where there is stiffness in your life, where things have stagnated and grown wasteful, is where you must begin to break yourself again. When you see that you are stuck on any given track, look around for disruptive events to shift you. There is always an unprepared-for something occurring nearby. It is the potential start of a new narrative pathway, away from the inadequate familiar and into the challenging unknown.

# 33
# Conflict and Ideology

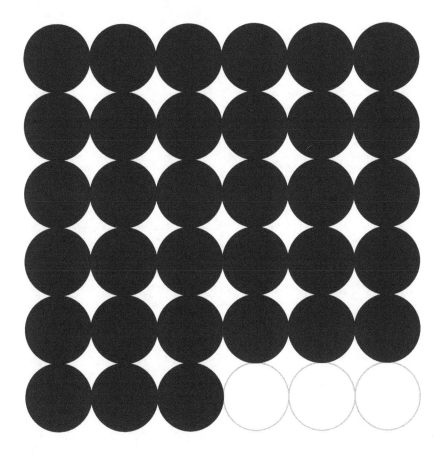

# Conflict and Ideology

*Heroism exemplifies the best of humanity's potential in some contagious manner, improving the social environment through its influence. We gradually reveal what the world could become, each of us embodying excellence in select domains appropriate to our natures. Once we are defined wholly by our values, it is our duty to uphold them through our anomalous perspective and abilities whenever they are threatened by nefarious human forces who have not attained a principled type of existence. And in doing so, we might just become something worthy of humanity's fickle admiration.*

———————◆———————

Every adventurer, from the time he enters the world unknown, navigates a landscape of competing ideologies and ideals. He falls into conflict with dominant paradigms not aligned with his own and must decide for himself what most to continue to care about out of all available options. Indeed, because the crux of the hero's maturation lies in accepting that there will always be aspects of reality that he cares about more than any other, if he should lack real confidence in his discernment about how to feel and believe, lesser minds will forever determine his aims for him instead. Without the will of others imposed upon him, he must arrive to grand conclusions about what he cares about via his own direct investigation. That is why he must become quite sensitive to his own nature, so that he can observe how different forms of experience affect him uniquely from the herd.

Those who do not choose their own character display no real agency throughout their lives. They become only vessels for dominant ideologies to enter and control. They have had their occupations handed down to them by those who came before. A person of no principle has no reliable character to speak of. There is no way to predict what he will do when his motivators shift with environment and circumstance. But a person of character remains the same inside, regardless of what goes on about him.

The heroic actor determines the meaning to his actions meticulously and accurately, no matter what he should encounter. Whenever he makes something tangible his goal, anything unrelated to the pursuit of it blurs before him. In an important way, what he sets his sights on shapes everything else about his identity, his actions, and his absolute place in the world. That is why he must be so careful about parsing through all the conflicting doctrines he is certain to encounter as he moves ever further from the simple place where he began.

Ideas, once implanted, naturally extend to other territories. They seek out the unilateral alignment of human thought to their objectives at the cost of personal perspective. Each of us, until we have surpassed our ideological trials, is vulnerable to the usurping of our values by countless competing others. If we inherit our values wholly from our culture, we cannot rely on self-assessment and internal evaluations about how reality works, what we ought to care about, and how we ought to behave in every circumstance. Only when we are rooted certainly in our principles do we grow immune to psychic interference.

Because thought creeds and doctrines bleed out from the minds around us and inevitably spill into our own, we are always facing some level of conflict and temptation about their second-hand influence. Surrendering to the strongest ideological influence in our environment absolves us of the responsibility of determining our own righteous behavior. It means we abdicate the liability of having to do something different, something heroic or unprecedented, when no one around us will because their institutional instructions do not allow them to. After all, ordinary people don't want to be the ones in charge of deciding how the most important moral issues of life will go down when human intervention in the downward flow of entropy actually matters, when every choice contributes to an important mythological outcome for us and our world.

When we are weak enough to let ourselves outsource our value hierarchies to cultural authorities, it means, essentially, that we do not trust our minds' abilities to interpret our experience with absolute and consistent meaning that will survive rigorous deconstruction and attacks. The battle for our attention goes forever unresolved because we do not hold ourselves accountable to what we allow into our minds. If we could only own our preferences and the invisible factors that lead us to see the world the ways we do, we would accept that it was our burden alone to manifest our principles through our conscious behavior, no matter how that would contradict what the world would prefer us to believe.

What do you become without the support of culture or convention to dictate your cares? Where does your integrity lie? Where do you stand or falter? What do you really aim for without external influence to make the determination for you? It is only when everything is working against you that you see how your priorities really are. What you will find when you are brave enough to look at what really delineates your action may shock and scare, for it may be quite far from the person you publicly and privately pretend you are.

Reality herself cares not at all about your newly uncovered heroic values. It is you alone who must make them matter out there. When something unsettles you about how people operate in the world, it is you who moves to rectify that primordial feeling of injustice. Will you act upon your perception of fundamental wrongness, the imbalance you perceive that causes ache within your soul, and put yourself at risk of harm or distress to bring resolution where it is not? Or will you step down from that exalted pedestal because you fear the existential investment it requires from you and the costs you may have to bear for embodying what you claim to believe in?

Heroism, despite popular depictions, is not only measured in the accomplishment of big important goals. It lies in how committed you are to yours and how courageous you must be to even attempt what you alone seem to know is worth caring about and defending from intruding conflict. Embodying extraordinary character necessitates looking beyond your base-level gratifications to see what is genuinely fundamental to your fulfillment. Accepting every consequence of your behavior becomes easy then, as nothing will be more important to you than remaining aligned with what you know is true and worthwhile about your identity.

So, you must be very careful about what you choose to aim your thoughts at when the world presents a smorgasbord of incompatible options. Whatever you seek for yourself will be what you eventually find, for you will ignore anything that comes before or beyond it. Your ideals also define your limitations and make all meaningful interactions between you and other humans possible. In time, you will be recognized for the things you stand for and the principles you never betray, but only if you have earned that place in the same way those principles have earned a place in you. If you have done your job right, the people who matter most to you in life will come to rely on you as the shining example you have finally uncovered yourself to be.

# 34
# Disillusionment and Reflection

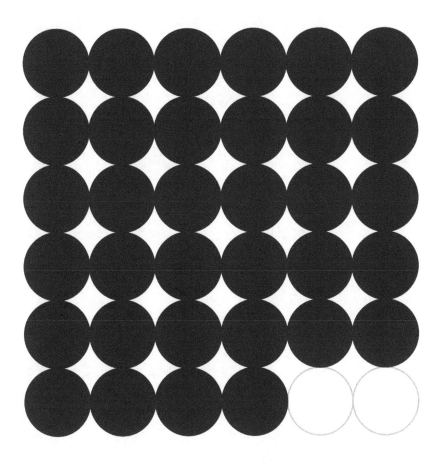

# Disillusionment and Reflection

*Without the capacity to endure significant discomfort, heroic values are totally useless in the world. Without toughness to persevere against real pain and friction, we can only imagine ourselves as champions of our values in the realm of our ideas. In the realm of the real, our actions always carry consequences, and we must place ourselves in the path to feel them and remain there until they've passed. We must retain the perspective to reflect on the hollow effects of disillusionment when our theories do not turn out to match our reality and integrate the necessary lessons, or else we never learn what it was that caused us to lose our once-unassailable motivation.*

◆━━━━━━━━━━━━●━━━━━━━━━●◆

As part of maturation is the realization of priorities, what necessarily follows is the actionable embodiment of them throughout every facet of one's being. Values, to mean anything at all, should be adopted as absolute principles that instigate and delineate all action in one's life. However, such a daunting prospect is impossible to perfectly execute by even the greatest of real-world heroes. No matter the effort exerted, there will always be some space between the standards one envisions and the actual ability to live. So, heroes must accept that they will never live up to their own principled standards.

No one has perfect control (or even a perfect understanding) of even himself, let alone the endless variables of his environment that affect his ability to live. As such, no one can be a perfect embodiment in action, only in spirit, will, and inspiration. The exceptional person tries as often and as hard as he needs to approach his ideals, despite forever falling short of his vision of them. He will never be as good as he imagines he should be, but that doesn't stop him from trying.

Such is the ongoing curse of the greatly ambitious. It is the wound that never fully closes: to be perpetually dissatisfied with oneself and have no other choice but to deal with it. Chronic dissatisfaction, especially if not softened by an adequate level of respect and reward for whatever progress one makes, leads to demotivation. Demotivation creates an eternal negative feedback loop, where it only grows easier and easier to continue to fall short of one's goals.

As a human being is both a thinking and feeling creature, he must use all aspects of his mind, including both his intellect and emotions, in total congruence with each other. His thoughts teach him to arrange reality to achieve his values, but they do not actually motivate his actions beyond providing a causal understanding of their nature and consequences. Emotions play that role, breaking inertia and providing the impulse to apply thoughts for new purposes. Chaos, in the end, cannot be navigated without the propulsion provided by emotion.

Every human strategy is predicated on the expectation of satisfaction from success or, alternatively, the opposite for failure. These emotional expectations tell us where to go and how to behave. Intellect is merely the mechanism that tells us how to get where inspiration moves us. That is why it is so important that we allow ourselves to directly witness the consequences of our actions and compare them with what our intentions were for the plans we put into motion. We need to always be ready to recalibrate what we expect to happen against what actually does.

We may, at times, still pride ourselves on our iron resolve, but resolve is not enough to live continuously in apt virtue. Our bodies are unavoidably subject to fatigue in our ongoing battles against disorder. Weakness may strike at any time in a thousand different forms if we are not cognizant of our natures and limitations. In our moments of deepest reflection, when we are most disillusioned with what we think that we are striving for, we will need to find the strength to think proactively about our situations and how we will recover from our falls.

If we cannot feel natural joy when we accomplish something that is, by our own analysis, heroically important, we will begin to feel detached from our missions and what they stand for. And, on the other hand, if we do not ever feel the defeat of failure, we will grow too arrogant to be effective, never changing from our mistakes or recognizing when we've strayed from the heroic path. Without the earned sensations of punishment and reward, we will come to believe that nothing can be done to further reality along the path toward our values or, even worse, that we can do no wrong as we attempt it.

Reason can extrapolate magnitudes beyond the understanding of the senses. Yet, we are still primal creatures with animalistic lower functions as the basis to our heroic higher selves. If our minds go long periods failing to see what they consider by their metrics to be progress, they slowly accept that nothing can be done to achieve the outcomes they desire and that our actions have been entirely absent meaning. Even if we can logically extrapolate valid intellectual reasons why what we're doing with our time still makes sense and is relevant to our goals, a drought of emotional support will make it impossible for us to continue. We will, quite simply, run out of motion.

It is essential to be passionate about your pursuits but not so hotheaded that you do not pause to savor the spoils of your efforts. Without a connection to your emotional center, you will become worn and frantic, which will ultimately negate your ability to do the things you consider to be so important to your sense of heroic identity. It is quite counterproductive to believe that your greatness depends upon chronic suffering and does not have room for catharsis. It is the same to believe that things will only ever work out as you plan and that you will never have to wallow in recognition of your vital errors.

Always, to remain upon the principled path of choice, you need those precious moments that restore you from the friction of loss and difficulty. The right stimulus at the right time will always have profound effects upon your will. Regular restoration counters disillusionment in the face of great adversity. As well, it would be best if you embraced the self-corrective mechanisms of guilt and reflection whenever you commit mistakes that lead to catastrophic failure. They are, after all, the only way to dissuade yourself from making the same mistakes again.

As you saunter between emotional differences, watch for consistency in what causes you to variate. Identify within yourself those specific experiences that return you to a state of feeling like yourself again, motivated for what moves you. It does not matter what type of activity it is or which of your senses it stimulates. Immerse yourself in the activities that reinvigorate your motivation to be part of the good in the world once more so that you can go out into the fray again and be it.

When the world seems overwhelming in its obstacles and its evil, reflect upon what challenges you have indeed overcome and the good you have been able to accomplish, even if it is not the overwhelming and absolute good you would like to claim. Remember who you used to be and how you used to act compared to the better person you are now. Reminisce about how far you have come and how important it is that you continue to hold the knowledge and light in an environment so dark and so oblivious to the problems you have the insight to observe.

# 35
## Demise and Rebirth

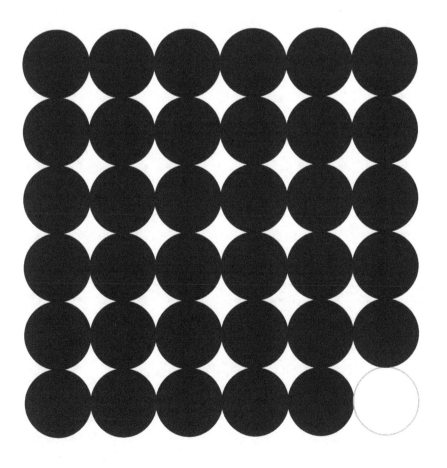

# Demise and Rebirth

*The false self, the adopted identity imposed by a corrupt world that relies on it in order to maintain its dysfunction, through ruthless deconstruction, will eventually die. But, after a period of aimlessness, experimentation, and discovery, the rules that dictate what we ought to do and who we ought to be come to seem wholly phony and without merit. Surpassing this point, we can feel good about sacrificing the ways we used to be and dedicate our lives to renewed order. We can remake ourselves in the heroic image we should have been aspiring toward from the start.*

◆─────────────●─────────────◆

An ordinary person is so reluctant to define himself that he allows the trajectory of his life to go wherever the most convenient available social narrative will take him. His accepted world carves out a ready place for him, and he is all too willing to let these prevailing forces tell him who he is supposed to be and what his life shall become within their setting. Never straying too far in any direction, he maintains barriers around his most vulnerable sensitivities in order to avoid anything more than a hint of agency or the injury that necessarily accompanies it.

The source of the primordial problem is that agency generally does not evolve in the individual until after they have already inherited social schematics for living in the world. Young people intuitively seek approval because social cohesion is necessary for their survival. So, they cultivate a handful of favorable traits that go on to define their place in the prevailing social order, and they do this at the cost of free and authentic self-discovery.

The misled person is condemned to spend his life chasing something inauthentic, a false ideal that was planted in him long before he realized that he could actually think for himself if he just willed himself to. That vision the world gave him protects him from straining too hard in any capacity. His cage becomes his home, for he knows no life and no identity beyond it. The voice he thinks is his own belongs to countless others, and it drowns out the lingering whispers of what he could have become and accomplished. This is a man who has never met himself, the man who dies, never having lived at all.

So long as he allows other people to define the rules and categories under which he interprets his world, he will never meet who he would feel most comfortable being. If he blindly embraces faith in incidental tradition, he will never look for emergent alternatives that would enable him to follow his genuine interest instead. In any case, even on the phony path, he will never be good enough by the standards of his world at being something he was not meant for. Upon reaching the critical step, the refusal to accept that life must proceed according to an unconsciously curated plan, the heroic individual can begin to express all the parts of himself that the world is not ready to contain. He must only slay the silent instructions the voices of the past left for him to follow about what is correct, what is allowed, and what is true.

Externally idealized versions of us get created the moment other people successfully project their preferences into our self-impressions. Most of the time, they do not even know that they are doing it. They do not recognize the influence they wield. When they identify something they like about us, they generate a feedback loop of positive reinforcement. We learn to desire their approval, so we artificially emphasize the qualities they favor in us above the rest. With enough social accolades, we will forfeit anything contradictory, anything that goes against what we have learned we are most celebrated for, amputating large swaths of our potential in the process. Duty to the illusion becomes the sticking point of our whole social existence.

Then, when we cease to believe in the illusion of who we were supposed to have been all along, our struggle will have finally just begun. People who play the most important roles in our lives will continue to conform us to what they know and value about us. They need us to continue to play by the rules of their world so that we are convenient to conceptualize and interact with. To walk away from their prepared spaces is to threaten their understanding of not only us but even themselves. Consequently, we cannot really explore ourselves so long as we remain characters in others' narratives. So long as we fear to lose the roles they play for us and we for them, they reign over us.

There is still hope of escape. The emotional awareness in you that wishes to no longer relegate your life to slavery and puppetry under unseen social forces grows increasingly discontent. At a critical point, you may finally be ready to lose the goodwill you have built over the course of your false life. Everything you have ever been is contained under the contextual filter of the person the world knows you to be, but that alone is no longer enough to sustain you. Now, it has become necessary for that person to die.

The world will always fight what it considers too different to integrate into its structures. The existence of outliers challenges its inhabitants, forcing them to consider that reality might be structurally different than they have grown comfortable assessing. They cannot help but lash out against whatever they perceive disrupts their foundations until even your most cherished familiar faces come to hate you on an existential level. Are you prepared for such a sacrifice?

It requires tremendous bravery to choose to live under conditions of existential uncertainty. Choice is always is the first step of heroism, even the choice to sacrifice everything you know yourself to be, to wake up from a dream into a reality where you cannot know what you will encounter. By embracing your own demise, you no longer need to carry the baggage of the person you were supposed to have been. You'll think independently and act for your own reasons, even if no one around you, no one you once relied on for survival and a sense of social distinction, can understand the mechanisms and destination of your agency.

Existential suicide is only the clearing away of space in your identity for something more true to grow than what previously occupied it. It is necessarily uncomfortable, but the lasting rewards are far greater than the required sacrifices. What necessarily follows every end for those who endure is always a new beginning that, through conscious effort, can be better than what was before. It is finally time to discover the new mode of being that should have been there all along in you had your natural development never been interrupted.

# 36
## Ideals and Spread

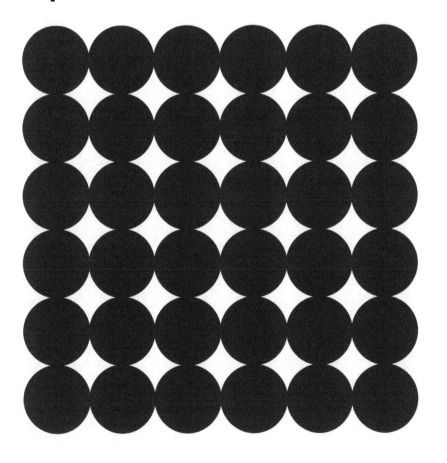

# Ideals and Spread

*Upon elimination of everything false about life, freedom at least from faulty narratives about who to be lie within reach. In following the natural course of destiny now identified, every step carries weight for us that was absent prior to our attainment of this timeless understanding. Every choice has its origin in our sacred ideals. Every justification is linked to the pursuit of a meaning that is deeper for us than any temporary satisfaction gleaned by our merely going along to get along, the default operating state of nearly everyone. What we do now is the final display of what we are and have always truly been made of.*

◆—————————•—————————◆

When evaluating the correct place in any situation, one must insist on wondering, "In what way can I accomplish the most good as I understand the term in an absolute and objective manner? In what way can I align myself most with what I now know to be true, important, and worthwhile in a cosmic and timeless sense?" Then, one cares less about what sacrifices and discomforts are required to resolve these vital questions and act in accordance with their answers.

There will be a great and irreplaceable reward when the purposeful mind sees, finally, that the world has changed, even a little, as a result of his self-derived actions. Things will then be a little closer to how he knows that he needs them to be, and there is no other feeling in the world available to humans that compares to that. In time, he will become so certain in his vision that he will even lay down his life, if necessary, to bring it to fruition or protect it from disruption by either natural accident or directed villainous attack.

Through maturation, a human being becomes less responsive and more proactive. The cessation of immediate aches, which once dominated almost all his actions, will take a back seat to principle and purpose, granting him greater endurance for disturbing experiences that once would have easily removed him from his path. He will not mind deep suffering so much, as he will, even in his darkest moments, relish in the deep spiritual reward that only comes via pursuit of his known priorities. When he is ready, he will rely hardly at all on events surrounding him to determine the good from the bad. He will know because he will be calm and intimately familiar with all the emotional processes affecting the chemistry of his thoughts and value judgments, not a reactionary piece of machinery any longer.

His extreme lows and highs will now seem intimate and connected. They are the forces that will drive his behavior, as all else will be seen as but mundane human distraction: unconscious voices fighting for space in a limited arena. More than that, he will become uncommonly aware of why he perceives the world the way he does. He will address each layer of his psyche, tearing it apart and piecing it together for optimal flow according to the purposes he has found. Living with this awareness is the difference between a fulfilling life and one of constant soul suffering.

We are destined to feel lost and empty for a time, not knowing in which direction to turn next because we will have given up on all our familiar bearings. The rules that once established where we ought to go will be seen to be phony, shallow, and no longer any useful. The only emotions that come now, beyond the basic requirements of our survival, the impulses that keep us alive and functioning, will be those that originate in the passions inherent to who we are, which is likely still a mostly barren concept for us because we have only just begun to live out the experiences necessary to populate it with meaning.

In fact, the goal of our journey has never been to acquire specific knowledge or ability, except to the extent that doing so might aid our ability to improve things. It has been to disentangle ourselves from disingenuous narrative biases so that we may begin to live as the optimally heroic versions of ourselves. It has been to learn to silence the voices that determined how information would be processed and the meaning held by us. If we can only do this, we will be finally free to make our meaning independently.

This is how we shall overcome the impossible obstacle inhibiting humanity from spontaneously developing: by contributing the parts that each of us is uniquely suited to embody and spread. To do this, we must recognize that as crucial as the ability to live and operate with independence is, our development cannot end with independence. It is just as necessary for us to empower others to step into their own self-reflection, resetting, and maturation as it was for others to help us form the realizations we certainly would have missed on our own. We are but only a small sample out of billions of cycles of perpetuating misdirection. The world needs so much more.

Perhaps the most difficult part of our task will be to enter the world self-aware, as internally aligned creatures who hold no wasteful connections to the past or any need to follow mindless instruction. Although the pursuit imparts a deep and lasting sense of purpose, it is not always kind to us nor enjoyable. It is, oftentimes, lonely but nonetheless essential, as we cannot go on living any other way. What all this time we may have been picturing as the end of the journey is revealed to be only yet another out of endless beginnings because the journey only ends when we expire.

Sooner or later, only what works will go on perpetuating on the planet. You will not know everything you are capable of until you challenge every limit the world gave you because it feared what you might one day become. When the present conflict is surpassed within you, only excellence remains, and that excellence is what is needed to move on from the present state of things that clearly does not work. The point of your personal evolution is to become a living part of the solution that will grant permanence to the exceptional traits that have accumulated within you through both the natural accident of your birth and the trials you have deliberately undertaken.

The endgame for every person identified with their values is to become a superhuman embodiment of those values. When you are ready, you will bring your sacred ideas out of your head and confirm them with all your actions. You will change your environment to be closer to your conception of or-

GREGORY V. DIEHL

der. You will become a guardian for that order, watching over it to protect it against any invading force that would seek to dismantle its structure to appease its own unaddressed insecurities, which is a trait that presently over-populates the planet. Thus, it is decidedly difficult to be a hero in the present unheroic age because you are still in a small but vital minority.

After you've eliminated everything false from your life, you are free from the chains of faulty ideals about who you were supposed to be. Search within yourself to garner a glimpse of the character you wish to be playing in your narrative. The world knows the name and face you wear, but it doesn't yet know the intangible values behind the mask that now can't help but bleed through. You will know where you stand and where you fall. You will know who you are because you will know what you must protect. The journey of your heroic development climaxes in the confrontation of your deepest fears and even possibly your literal death. On the other end of such confrontation is the truest version of you that does not rely on the psychological supports of the phony world to maintain appearances of sanity and virtue.

# DENOUEMENT

## A Champion of and for Reality and Self

I don't have much space in my time left as a living part of this world for most of the empty experience that humans seem preoccupied with, as most of it is not real or relevant for longer than it takes to surmount a fleeting weakness or obstacle. I know that my superficial burdens do not define me. The way the people I happen to have known until now prefer to categorize me is not the extent of what I am, if it is even accurate at all. Collective ideals about how life ought to be structured and values prioritized pass over and around me mostly too fast to even notice, let alone adopt and integrate.

As much is clear to me that I have always been on a different path, working toward something utterly more than what seemed to be available. What was not always clear was whether the sacrifices required to pursue, let alone achieve, what I want would be worth it, if I could endure the longing and alienation long enough for some proportionate reward to arise as a result of my dedication to ideals. But no matter my stamina or the strength of my will, I could never willingly return to a state of ignorance over my own nature and that of the world I was stuck in.

The heroic path timelessly referred to is the one that leads out of illusion and into reality. It is a path that has no end because I can never know that I have reached an absolute and permanent acquisition of the truth about reality or myself. It is all I can do to surrender myself to moving further still at every stage, to devote myself to serving what is revealed to be real and embodying the totality of what I am in my behavior.

In embracing this purview, I find that so much of what once occupied my mind and time swiftly fades. I see that most of the pursuits of my past hardly mattered at all to the values I confidently hold now. Almost none of my relationships were based on anything principled or substantial. They were almost all the products of automatically reacting to environmental factors I had no capacity to distance myself from and analyze the rightness and righteousness of. So how could there ever have been a real choice in the matter?

Choice is a terrible burden. It carries not only the obvious responsibility of its outcomes but also the understated responsibility of the emotional state and knowledge necessary to the act of making a choice in a non-arbitrary manner. Few have the drive or ethic of self-development to undertake these dual responsibilities. Fewer still can endure the effects of their failure in applying them enough times to learn from their mistakes and grow more adept at wielding them. To continue, even when it seems you are the only one in the world with the natural drive to make such meaningful choices, is the most heroic thing I or you can do with our lives.

Now and at the end of all things, I know, without hesitation, which side of the dichotomy between truth and illusion I align to, to the best of my imperfect ability, until the time that I expire. I know this because to gain this reasonable self-confidence became a desire more powerful for me than any superficial emotional trigger, anything that might become a blind spot to living in accordance with my deepest nature. None of this is to suggest that I do not still have my triggers that function to momentarily pull my focus off of what is real and most essential according to my inborn sense of purpose. It's only that I never lose perspective of seeing them for what they are: Obstacles arising from a still-unoptimized human psyche. They are my companions, but they can never again become my masters and divert me into living as a fraudulent version of myself. Reality is my only god now, a god that is forever unknowable and just beyond the reach of all my striving.

What remains when all artificiality and illusion have been threshed away by the processes of inward examination and outward trials is just the self and the reality it inhabits, and that is all I should ever really hope for. There was only ever one decision to make from the beginning of my conscious life until now: To live in accordance with my nature or rebel against it due to any of countless forms of latent insecurity. The whole of everything here has been communicated with only the purpose of moving me and you further along the path to the point that the choice now comes, well, naturally, so that we will continue to make it at every difficult juncture in life. May we always resist the empty temptation to sacrifice heroic principle for passing comfort.

The question may nonetheless remain: Why? Why take on the burden of holding such a grand perspective about my place, my life, and the importance I imbue into every action? Almost anyone can momentarily achieve the hero's perspective in an inspired moment, but it disappears just as quickly. Isn't it enough just to go along and get along? To live, let live, and avoid harming anyone as you go? To not be actively malevolent or destructive, so long as you don't get in the way?

The answer is as simple as the question: No. No, it is not enough. It will never be enough, not for people like us. If it were any other way, we wouldn't be here having this conversion right now. Ours is a dialogue for those who have always needed more, those who suffer because mere adequacy is inadequate. I feel pain not for being a problem or a burden in this world, an overtly evil character who demands redemption for his awful crimes, but for lacking narrative mythological purpose to my life. Put plainly: I am not living the life I know I ought to. But I'm getting closer.

Now the only question that remains for me and you is that of whether we will choose to remain true to ourselves when it is difficult until it is difficult no longer, until life and its automatic processes are arranged to service the most glorious possible forms of us. Or will you and I take the path of the utter majority and surrender to the entropic river, reality's tendency toward disorder? Will our distinction from the norm disappear back into it just as quickly as it appeared and well before it ever had the chance to become noteworthy? To do so would seem to be the easy choice, but in time, we may find that it becomes a great amount more intolerable than whatever resistance we face in choosing the heroic alternative.

Awareness, once lit, is not so easy to snuff out in the anomalous individual, even after years of attempting to dull it through mundane thoughts and experience. As the perception that stems from it cannot ever fully be ignored, the only reasonable choice is to fully commit to the embrace of myself as I really am and, by extension, reality as she really is. But to walk that path requires the constant development of great new characteristics and the activation of all my latent potential. It puts me on an internal journey that tests me in ways that mundane obstacles never could, including emotional conflicts that previously could not have existed in me. With a deeper mode of living comes, unavoidably, a deeper experience of life.

It's a strange sort of paradox. I know that nothing I do really seems like it could be all that objectively important. Yet, choosing to live fully in accordance with my nature and hold myself to the highest possible standard is the most important thing that I could ever do, as it determines everything else about the totality of my existence. It is the prime mover of my humanity. The choice to learn in a mythological way about myself and how I will continue to live while I am here makes all the difference in the world.